Experiencing Special Educational Needs and Disabilities

GW00673657

Experiencing Special Educational Needs and Disabilities

Lessons for Practice

Brahm Norwich

 Open University Press

Open University Press
McGraw-Hill Education
8th Floor
338 Euston Road
London
NW1 3BH

email: enquiries@openup.co.uk
world wide web: www.mheducation.co.uk

and Two Penn Plaza, New York, NY 10121-2289, USA

First published 2017

A catalogue record of this book is available from the British Library

ISBN-13: 978-0-33-526246-5
ISBN-10: 0-33-526246-5
eISBN: 978-0-33-526247-2

Library of Congress Cataloging-in-Publication Data
CIP data applied for

Typeset by Transforma Pvt. Ltd., Chennai, India

Fictitious names of companies, products, people, characters and/or data that may be used herein (in case studies or in examples) are not intended to represent any real individual, company, product or event.

Printed and bound by CPI Group (UK) Ltd, Croydon, CR0 4YY

Praise for this book

"A critical part of understanding any complex social phenomenon is to listen (really listen) to the views of the stakeholders – the children and young people, the parents and the professional educators. In this thoughtful book, Brahm Norwich, a leading scholar in the field of Disability and Special Educational Needs, faithfully presents these views through 12 insightful case studies. The stories told are direct and share the tensions, dilemmas, balances and dynamics of life. It is a very thought-provoking book and an excellent addition to the field."

Dr Graeme Douglas, Professor of Disability and Special Educational Needs, University of Birmingham, UK

"An invaluable book about the importance of getting to know each and every child, comprising up to date case studies that contextualise the experiences of 12 learners identified with special educational needs."

Professor Lani Florian, Bell Chair of Education, University of Edinburgh, UK

"In the era of person-centred planning, this book is a timely and essential key text for both general and specialist practitioners working for children and young people with special educational needs and/or disability. The structured case study format provides accessible, comprehensive and detailed insights across a range of ages and types of educational placement. Whilst evidence from the individual experiences of children, their families and teachers are its main substance, the book also draws together case study themes, including advice directly given by parents and teachers to the readers. Professor Norwich is to be highly commended for providing this original, scholarly and useful research to the international field of special education."

Professor Kevin Woods, Professor of Educational and Child Psychology, University of Manchester, UK

"In his new book of 12 case studies of children and young people with a range of special educational needs and disabilities (SEND), Brahm Norwich skilfully presents the perspectives of the young people themselves, their parents, and the teachers and teaching assistants who support them. These careful, illuminating accounts bring to life the realities, complexities, challenges - and also the positive aspects - of the young people themselves and those that care and support them. They remind us all of the importance of seeing each child as an individual. Required reading for all who work with children with SEND."

Professor Geoff Lindsay, Centre for Educational Development, Appraisal and Research (CEDAR), University of Warwick, UK

Contents

Acknowledgements

I would like to thank all those who participated in the case studies – parents, children and young people, teachers and teaching assistants who cannot be named. I hope the accounts reflect your experiences and views faithfully.

Many thanks to colleagues who read and commented on draft case studies: George Koutsouris, Margie Tunbridge, Sam Carr, Hazel Lawson and Ella Norwich. Many thanks also to Harriet Seddon and Elizabeth Dodsworth for their interview transcriptions. And thanks to Clara Norwich for prompting me to write a book in this style.

1

Introduction

Mother of a young person with special educational needs (SEN): 'Some people can be absolutely incredible, but at other times some people just don't want to know or genuinely don't understand.'

Why this book?

This book was written as an introduction to the special needs and inclusive education field for teachers, teaching assistants and other allied professionals, e.g. speech and communication therapists, educational and clinical psychologists, as well as policymakers and parents. It represents the experiences of a set of parents, teachers, teaching assistants and children/young people with identified special educational needs and/or disabilities from an educational perspective. It does so by aiming to illustrate some of their experienced tensions and issues and how they dealt with them. In doing so, it might also act as a reminder to more experienced professionals in the field about current practices, systems and policies. The basic aim of the book is to promote empathy, in the sense of expanding the capacity to understand the experiences of special educational needs from the perspective of those directly involved.

A brief note is needed about the use of terms. The phrase special educational needs and disability is used throughout the chapters because this is the current way of talking in England, not because these are the most suitable or justifiable terms. The final chapter illustrates some of the varied perspectives about the terms used and the system of identification and category use.

The book consists of a series of case study reports based on interviews (mostly taking place in 2015) with parents, teachers or teaching assistants, and children or young people covering a wide range of special educational needs. The purpose of the book is to give a broad perspective on the range of difficulties and disabilities to compare and contrast the views and experiences of parents, teachers/assistants and the children/young people themselves in their own terms. The main point of this is to bring out positive experiences as well as negative ones so that the reader can see what is involved in positive models of practice and can be aware of negative practices to avoid.

The reason for presenting case studies using the words of the participants is to give a feel for these complex, contrary and challenging experiences. Some people do not want to know, or genuinely do not understand, as one of the participating mothers put it, as expressed in the initial excerpt of this chapter. There are reasons for these stances, but to understand these reasons the basic experiences need to be presented and understood.

One of my main reasons for writing this book was to contribute to the professional learning of teachers and other allied professionals. With the adoption of a more inclusive education perspective in this country and internationally, there has been much emphasis on preparing all teachers – not just those specialising in special educational needs – to be more aware of special educational needs and disabilities and to adopt more positive attitudes to teaching and supporting children with these additional needs. The parents who participated in the study were told that their involvement in the study was a way in which they could communicate to those undergoing initial and continuing professional development.

I have been involved in teacher education and conducted research for many years. Based on this experience I have drawn some conclusions about professional learning needs. One conclusion has been that the learning of the attitudes and values of respect and caring for all is a central part of preparing those who are to work and support children and young people with SEN and disabilities. Another conclusion has been that respect and caring, especially for those who are different from the norm, is more challenging in a social context where those with disabilities and difficulties of all kinds struggle for affirmation and respect, and require flexibility of practices and provision. One way to prepare teachers, that has been tried in this country, has been to provide opportunities to observe and teach children and young people with special educational needs and disabilities in separate and ordinary settings – by direct and personal practical experience. Though there is no substitute for such direct experience, there is also a place for in-depth and integrated accounts of people's experiences of special educational needs and disabilities. These accounts not only illustrate practices and procedures but support the emotional and value education which is also an important part of preparing to work with these children and young people and their parents.

The 12 case studies making up the book are written in a narrative and descriptive style. They do not present authoritative professional-research positions about the latest knowledge and understanding in the field, nor present general guidance about how to practise. There are other current books which present broad views about how parents can understand their child with special needs. Some combine a mixture of professional-research knowledge about diagnosis, treatment, therapy, education and family relationships. Other books focus on specific areas such as autism or Down Syndrome. There are books written by parents which give detailed accounts of the parenting of a child with a complex set of needs, and the administrative and legal battles involved in securing appropriate provision for their child. There is also a kind of book which provides guidance about strategies for professionals working with parents of children with special educational needs. With the new SEN/disability legislation in England, there are also guidance books for SEN coordinators and trainee teachers. There are also books that capture the perspectives and experiences of parents and/or professionals in the field, but do so either to advocate for a particular position – for example, inclusive schools, or as the basis for an academic analysis of inclusive education for a particular area of disability. This particular book is different from all these kinds of books, and can be seen to complement them.

Case studies and organization of the book

The 12 case studies have been selected to represent, as far as was practically possible during the study period, a variety of situations, children and families. All children and young people had Statements of special educational needs; only one had been issued with an Education, Health and Care Plan (EHC Plan). Table 1 below shows a mix of age, stage of education and gender. It was decided to limit the age range to school- and college-going pupils or students, so it did not include those below 5 years old and those in higher education. Though this is not in keeping with the expanded age range of the new English special educational needs and disability (SEND) legislation (0–25 years), it was done for practical reasons. The areas of special educational needs are defined in terms of broad areas current in the SEN Code of Practice (DFE, 2014b):

   i. Social emotional and mental health difficulties.
  ii. Cognition and learning.
 iii. Communication – interaction.
  iv. Sensory-physical.

These specific areas of SEND are used because they are current, not because they are seen as the most effective ways of defining or classifying the range and types of functioning or need. Similarly, the specific categories used are the ones current in the SEN Code of Practice and represent the primary areas of SEN/disabilities. As each case study will show, the difficulties of some children and young people could not be captured by a simple set of primary areas of need. The case studies also show participants have their views about the use and value of categories like this. The third aspect of the cases selected is their educational placement. There is a range of ordinary provision, primary and secondary schools, some of which have units or centres specializing in specific aspects of SEN/disability; special schools, alternative provision (separate settings), ordinary and special further education colleges; and combined (ordinary and separate special settings) and co-located placement (special school co-located with ordinary school). The fourth aspect was about family and demographic background. There were variations in the social-economic position of parents and the rural–urban location of where they lived. However, there was less variation in the ethnic background of participants which did not meet the expected level of variation sought in the study design.

Table 1 Overview of case studies: age, gender, areas of SEN and school placement.

	Name*	Age	Gender	Areas of SEN		Placement
1	Marian	8	Girl	Cognition and learning	Moderate learning difficulties	Primary
2	Sharon	9	Girl		Severe learning difficulties	Special school
3	Ben	12	Boy		Severe learning difficulties	Primary – special school co-located with secondary school
4	Steve	14	Boy		Specific learning difficulty	Secondary school and unit
5	Jon	6	Boy	Social emotional and mental health difficulties (SEMH)	SEMH	Alternative provision
6	Sandy	12	Girl		SEMH	Residential special school
7	Tom	7	Boy	Communication – interaction	Speech difficulties	Primary and unit
8	Alex	10	Boy		Autistic spectrum disorder	Primary
9	Nina	18	Girl		Autistic spectrum disorder/ Moderate learning difficulties	Special further education college
10	George	5	Boy	Sensory-physical	Visual impairment	Secondary school
11	Julia	14	Girl		Physical disabilities	Secondary school
12	Tricia	18	Girl		Hearing impairment	Special school and further education college

*Anonymised names.

This set of case studies focuses more on breadth and depth, and less on being nationally representative. Nevertheless, it is a unique and contemporary set of case studies that can convey and shed light on the views, feelings and experienced issues of those who live with special educational needs in a contemporary UK (England).

Each case study is written in terms of the following sections:

1   *Quotes from participants*: advice to others based on their experiences.
2   *Background information*: personal details, where the child or young person lives and is at school/college; who was interviewed and where.
3   *Identification of SEN/disability*: strengths and difficulties, diagnoses, relevant history, impact on child and parents, labels and others' reactions and Statement details.
4   *Curriculum and pedagogy*: current and past educational provision, adaptations, what is important to learn, how specialized are programmes, learning progress and what helps/hinders learning, and teachers and teaching assistant details.
5   *Placement*: where is the child/young person at school or college, how they came to be there and decisions involved, outside school activities and inclusion/ exclusion beliefs.
6   *Parental involvement*: how parents relate to teachers and other professionals, disagreements and support groups/networks.
7   *Social interactions*: how children and young people interact with others in school and at home, friends and peers.
8   *Future*: perspectives on immediate and longer-term future; hopes and fears experienced.

The case studies centred round the parents' perspectives and experiences as the studies were started by making contact with parents, who then identified a teacher or teaching assistant who they considered best understood their child in a school or college setting. It was the parents who involved their children in the study too. The studies were written by comparing the three sets of interviews for each case covering the above areas. This provided a common framework within which the individual circumstances and characteristics of each case emerge (see appendix for more details).

Who the book is for and how it might be read and used

This book was initially written primarily for a broad education audience. It will be suitable for teachers in initial training and continuing professional development as an introduction to those who are new to the special needs and inclusive education field. But it might also be suitable to the initial training and education of allied professionals (those mentioned at the start of this chapter), including teaching assistants who work with children with special educational needs and disabilities.

This book will also be relevant to those teachers undertaking an SEN coordinator training course, as well as others undertaking advanced courses and Masters programmes in education. Given the central role of parents in the case studies, and their involvement in the design of the studies, the book might also be interesting to parents in general and those who have children with special educational needs and disabilities.

As the book is organised into separate chapters for each case study, and each case has a similar set of organising section headings, you can compare specific aspects across different case studies – for example, attitudes to labelling. You can also read specific chapters, depending on your interest – for example, the two cases relating to autism. If you are less interested in categories or areas of special educational needs, you can compare specific sections across each case – for example, placement and decisions about placement for one broad dimension, such as cognition and learning case studies. The case studies might also be relevant to short- and longer-term courses for trainee teachers or trainee SEN coordinators, where the focus could be across several key aspects – for example, identification and curriculum and pedagogy.

What follows this introductory chapter is the set of case study reports, which are organized in the four broad areas of SEN as numbered in the table above. They cover the four dimensions: Cognition and learning; Social emotional and mental health difficulties (SEMH); Communication – interaction and sensory-physical. Within each set the cases are organized by increasing age. The final chapter involves an analysis of the advice given by parents and teachers to others, and a summary of the key points and issues that arise from comparing the cases in terms of some of the themes in the study. In the second part of the final chapter there are also some links made to current research and policy to set the book in its wider context.

2
Marian

Mother: 'Be prepared to be disliked, be prepared to think differently, be prepared to think outside the box, be prepared to be a rebel. You have to have a sense of humour; don't be frightened of laughing at things, even if it feels quite dark. All you can ever do is just do your best, and that's all as much as any of us could ever do.'

Overview

Marian, who is 8 years old, lives with her mother and older brother (18 years old). She attends a local primary school in a rural area. Marian was interviewed at school in the presence of the SEN coordinator, and her mother was interviewed at home. An advisory teacher for children with communication and interaction difficulties was also interviewed, rather than the SEN coordinator, as the head teacher did not wish her to take part in the study.

Identification of needs

Difficulties and strengths

Marian's mother describes her as a 'complex child' who presents at first to most people as a 'typical child', similarly to other children with hidden disabilities. Marian's mother stated that due to her daughter's brain injury she could present as having behaviour similar to children with Attention Deficit Hyperactivity Disorder (ADHD), and that her communication style is similar to that of children on the autistic spectrum in that Marian can respond to situations in a very literal way: as her mother put it, Marian 'does not get it socially. She finds it very difficult to discriminate between people and their behaviour.' Her mother felt that Marian was overly trusting of people. She also said her daughter has physical disabilities, weakness in her hands and legs as well as cognitive issues and sensory issues – none of which are huge in themselves, but when combined form a significant disability. As her mother explained, 'all this makes it very difficult for Marian as she cannot excel at anything that might compensate for her other deficits'.

Although the advisory teacher had only recently become involved in advising about Marian, she had read the previous professional reports and referral details and had observed Marian in school. Her particular focus on Marian was her speech and language, but her assessment went beyond this focus. She believed that the key issue for Marian in a mainstream classroom was her working memory – 'her ability to build on from one piece of learning to another'. Her view was that appropriate support would enable her to make links between different learning experiences, so she could access the lessons.

The advisory teacher also commented that Marian was very fluent in her spoken language and able to explain when she could link back to her personal experience. However, when Marian was working with something more abstract not linked to her own experience, it was very hard for her. It is interesting that the advisory teacher did not feel that she could comment about her behaviour, though she noted that Marian's behaviour was 'impeccable' in the session and when observed 'she was working extremely well with the learning support assistant or in a group'.

Her mother also described Marian as 'totally persistent and she doesn't let things stop her, to the point that she will indulge in risk-taking behaviour'. She described her as very outgoing and thriving on social situations: 'she really wants to be in these very social settings, but she does have problems in coping with it'. However, her mother also explained how Marian was 'going through the process of becoming aware of her discrepancies and in some ways she's absolutely determined not to be different'. This is about her awareness of being behind others in her literacy and numeracy. She was working two to three years behind her expected levels, something also noted by the advisory teacher.

When Marian described herself, this was mainly in terms of her age and appearance – 'a little girl' with 'short hair' – adding that she was growing it longer. She focused then on her 'sense of humour' and that her teacher would say 'she worked very good'. Her friends, she thought, would say that she was 'good, happy and had a nice sense of humour'. She then added that 'when I was little I had a brain injury'. But, when asked to say more about the brain injury she turned to talking about a recent episode at the skateboard park when she fell over.

Causes

Her mother explained that Marian had a normal birth and did not present with any developmental issues until she was 4 years old. She went into a coma, which they assumed was meningitis B, and was taken to a local hospital. At that stage they thought she was about to die, and her mother felt that they were preparing her for Marian's death. Also, Marian did not respond to any medication related to meningitis or other sorts of encephalitis. She was eventually taken to a national centre some distance from where she lived, where they identified an acute disseminated encephalitis. Her mother explained that this was basically the same family as multiple sclerosis, and very rare. Marian's brain had suffered inflammation and this resulted in her acquired brain injury. With little knowledge about this rare condition, and acquired brain injury being so individual, the medical professionals adopted a trial and error approach. However, her mother believed that 'it's quite clear now that she is presenting with issues that are likely to be lifelong'. How her brain injury shows at present relates to how the advisory teacher identified Marian's difficulties in learning. She identified a speech and language element to her difficulties, but also a moderate learning difficulty element. By this she meant difficulties of a conceptual type which might be related to her working memory difficulties.

What followed the disseminated encephalitis

Marian was released after spending about a month in a hospital rehabilitation unit. She was barely verbal, needed lifting and handling, was doubly incontinent and needed feeding. Her mother felt that once Marian was discharged from hospital they were 'effectively abandoned by all the services'. Since then, Marian has made a 'remarkable recovery' for someone who was in such a deep coma for so long; there was no suggestion that she had suffered global damage. However, professional opinion has changed making it hard to have clear expectations about the near future. At first they suggested that she could make a complete recovery, but since then her mother had been told that this view was probably too ambitious. Marian was monitored for a year by a community paediatrician to see if there might be a relapse. This meant that she might at any time have needed an emergency hospital admission. But having gone for four years without a relapse, it is now considered to be a 'monophasic event' (occurring just once). Her mother explained that the professionals 'won't be interested unless she actually starts to exhibit any specific symptoms'.

Her mother described how the local community where they live was partly in shock when it happened because they thought it was meningitis. As there was a public health scare, Public Health contacted the nursery to address the concern that there was an emerging meningitis cluster as another child had recently been hospitalized for meningitis from the same nursery. The nursery staff were really supportive, and even people who did not know her sent Marian gifts.

Impact on family

Her mother explained that the impact of the brain injury on Marian was '24/7'. Marian was described as being aware of some aspects of her condition, but not others; this was partly about her only being 8 years old. But, she was 'becoming aware of it, it's very painful for her'. Her mother also felt that this was partly about the way that the school treated her: describing it as 'it could be a lot worse, but it's not brilliant'. Her mother also thought that Marian coped by denial: 'she'll say, "I don't want to talk about that mummy"'. Her mother's approach was to say that they would talk about it one day.

Marian's mother saw the impact of her acquired brain injury on her schooling and her experiences at school as enormous, 'not something that would go away'. Marian was described specifically as noticing that she was behind others in class in her literacy and numeracy and finding it very painful to talk about. Her mother felt that 'we can't just pretend it doesn't happen – which is what she would prefer'. The advisory teacher also observed that Marian was aware of having problems in learning.

Her mother explained that she had had a career in the disability independence movement and had worked for disability-led organizations. She felt that without that experience, she 'would not have been able to have coped as well because, on one level, although what's happened is very sad, it doesn't actually bother me at all . . . because I know already that a lot of people can get by in life and actually do really well and not actually be able to read or write very well'. She also explained that she had to work very hard to deal with her own feelings about Marian's circumstances. Sometimes she becomes very irritated when Marian does things 'that are just downright naughty'. She felt that Marian has to have boundaries like every other child. But, on the other hand, she felt that, as her mother, she needed 'to present a safe space for her, so she was able to experience her own unhappiness'. From what Marian's mother expressed, this seemed to be very challenging.

Marian's mother described how the older brother was devastated by what had happened. He had his own life now, studying A levels and about to go to university. He was described as being 'very good with her'. Marian saw her father about every six weeks. Marian, when interviewed, was just about to spend the next weekend with him and was looking forward to this. However, her mother described how her family had been 'absolutely useless' and she no longer had any contact with them because 'they let me and my daughter down really badly'.

Labels and others' responses

Her mother reported that the school's SEN coordinator did not use categories when talking to her about Marian, but from her own perspective she saw Marian as having 'cognitive issues, learning difficulties, physical difficulties, sensory processing . . . she's got a bit of everything that amounts to a whole lot'. Categories were used more as shorthand to describe patterns of behaviour rather than clear diagnoses. For example, when Marian was described as having 'poor concentration, disinhibition, inappropriate behaviour', she was described as 'more ADHD'. The advisory teacher also referred to cognitive difficulties when referring to a moderate learning difficulty, but she also identified what she called a 'speech and language communication element'.

An incident in a hospital car park was described when somebody shouted at Marian and her mother for parking in a disabled bay. Though Marian has a Blue Badge permitting them to park in the bay, her disability is hidden, and this person assumed they should not. Her mother also explained that one of the big problems is that some assume that Marian's mood swings and tantrums in public are due to poor parenting; 'Oh well – it has to be your parenting.' Marian can also be 'very lively and she's overfamiliar', and this can present her mother with problems. However, all this contrasts with the responses of those in the local area who know Marian: 'I'm very grateful to my neighbours who have been fantastic – absolutely fantastic – and very supportive.' Even at the local supermarket the staff are very friendly and entertain her when they go shopping. Her mother also explained that when Marian 'is in a routine and things are calm in her life she does not present issues'.

Statement

Marian was issued with a Statement without delay. Her mother felt that the local authority had behaved in a way that caused her no worries. The Statement had a full-time teaching assistant support associated as part of the special education provision. Getting the school to carry out the Statement details was her mother's concern. There have been regular annual reviews of Marian's SEN and at the most recent one they considered whether Marian would benefit from being identified as having a learning difficulty. This was also being discussed with health professionals. However, since the last review, her mother had not received the paperwork. This was because it had also been decided to amend the Statement to enable Marian to stay on another year when in year 6 (last year of primary school) after she reached that age. Her mother supported this decision because 'she's a year behind'.

There were plans to convert the Statement into the new Education, Health and Care (EHC) Plans later in the year. Though Marian's mother had not been briefed about the details of the new Plan, she believed that it would be more detailed than the Statement, because she 'will make sure of that'. But, the issues were as before: 'getting the school to implement it. It's also getting the backup from (the support services).'

Marian's mother also explained how, through her previous work with adults with disabilities, she came to be sceptical about the actual workings of the official system. She felt that local authorities can generally show a lack of political will and this was evident in her experiences with Statements/EHC Plans. She saw the advantages of Statements/Plans as part of a wider statutory framework that provides guidance and is enforceable. But she felt that the new SEN/disability legislation was rushed through too fast, and was too unwieldy: 'there is major distrust of parents' and 'I think it's not enforceable, there's not the finances'. She also felt that there was a degree of 'antipathy and ambivalence towards disabled people, both children and adults'. For her, what was going on in the adult area was indicative of whether there would be meaningful implementation of the new EHC Plans. As she explained, 'if there wasn't a Statement, she (Marian) wouldn't be attending school at all'.

Mental health

Marian's mother had battled with the local Child and Adolescent Mental Health Services (CAMHS), since Marian came out of hospital, over her behavioural problems. Despite the challenging nature of Marian's behaviour, the policy of the CAMHS was that parents had to attend a parenting course regardless of the circumstances. Marian's mother initially refused the course. But she then realized that this was a way to help; as she explained, 'I gritted my teeth and complied.' Though she thought that the course was well done and she enjoyed being with the other parents, she felt it was 'incredibly insulting that you have a child who has a very clear diagnosis, where there are no child protection issues, there's no cause for concern around the child, and the first thing they say to you is: "It's your parenting and you have to do a parenting course."' She explained that the CAMHS thinking was that because a social worker had been briefly involved around the time of the hospital stay, she was lacking as a parent. So, when Marian came out of hospital the local services had a 'level of suspicion around you being a parent that was horrendous; it's shocking'. The CAMHS service eventually concluded that Marian's behaviour problems were 'neurological and they now have got support for Marian's low self-esteem and anxiety'.

Learning: what and how

Education provision

The advisory teacher had observed Marian in the general class in a group working with others. Though the group had children with different abilities, what she was doing was differentiated to her individual level. Marian was observed doing literacy activities when she was coping well. Word maps and additional resources were available for her, such as a talk card, which recorded what she said, so she could hear it again – a way of supporting her memory. The advisory teacher reported that she was impressed with the teaching assistant's skills and how she knew when to become involved and when to leave her to work with the child next to her. Marian was observed to be familiar with the resources and to be supported in using these resources independently.

Marian's mother explained that Marian managed to cope with everyday demands at nursery school, but once she got to primary school things became complicated. At primary school Marian's teachers do not tell her what strategies are being used; 'I wanted to see a list of what strategies are in place (e.g. like precision teaching) and I thought that was meant to go on the Individual Education Plan (IEP)'. The lack of a written IEP was partly, she felt, about the SEN coordinator not doing the paperwork.

She knew that Marian was withdrawn from class for a small group activity, but there was a lack of clarity about that too. She realized that Marian presented the school with 'really complex issues' as she does not fit into what they are used to as regards SEN – e.g. ADHD or autistic spectrum. One response she has had about Marian is: 'She's got what?' The problem, as her mother saw it, was that many in the support services did not understand what to do; 'the school actually needs the support, but on the other hand they also need somebody to actually make them do it . . . that's a management issue'. For Marian's mother this was about the head teacher's weak management. Some parents, she reported, were baffled that a recent Ofsted inspection did not identify these issues, even though she knew that other parents had written to Ofsted at the time of the inspection about these matters.

Her mother believed that precision teaching had helped Marian to recognize whole words 'rather than doing constant phonics all the time'. But, overall she felt that Marian had not made much progress and wondered if this might be because she is unhappy at school: 'it is difficult to judge because she is school refusing'. These were big issues for her mother as most days there is a struggle, but she manages to get Marian into school nevertheless. She attributed the refusing to Marian's anxiety about being in school and other pupils' comments about her. Though Marian in interview with me did not talk about others' response to her, she did say that she needed a 'lot of help' with her reading and writing; 'I'm not very good at reading or writing because . . . I just get it all wrong sometimes because I was in hospital for a very long time.'

Educational needs

When Marian worked with the advisory teacher alone outside the class she needed to have the learning tasks broken into quite small chunks and then followed by a relaxation breather activity. Sustaining attention for a long period of time was hard for her. What was required was a balance between in-class learning with others around and short bursts of intensive withdrawal activity. The advisory teacher believed that Marian had very good language role models, so it was positive for her to be in a mainstream setting.

The advisory teacher talked further about the advice she gave about Marian's needs. Marian needed to become familiar with working in particular ways, to use tools consistently to support her learning numeracy and vocabulary. The advisory teacher's main advice was therefore about using concrete resources that Marian could use consistently to build on her knowledge. This advice was about avoiding the presentation of learning tasks in different ways as she was likely to have difficulties linking those experiences. When Marian came across an unfamiliar word she would use her experience to try to retrieve a word. The advisory teacher gave the example of Marian's response to the word 'balcony'. Marian could say that 'there's one of them at home, I walk up the stairs and I hold on to the. . .', but she could not retrieve the word. Her approach was to look at what linked with the word, but that takes much effort. So, the advice was to support her with vocabulary mapping and linking her phonological awareness (knowing the sounds) of that word to her semantic understanding (the meaning) of the word using some concrete means.

From her mother's perspective, Marian had 'distinctive needs'. She recognized that 'to be fair . . . it's borderline whether she should be in mainstream anyway'. This was because her mother believed that Marian's 'needs are outside really what mainstream can offer'. Drawing on her own experience of going to a school with a different ethos and approach, she was aware that there are other ways of educating children. So she wanted an 'alternative provision that is less focused on targets and literacy'. Her view was that if Marian was going to read, 'she will do it in her own time', so she wanted a school that focused more on social competencies. This was because 'in some ways her education focuses on her deficits rather than her abilities, and I think it's detrimental to her emotional and mental health'.

Her mother's views about the similarity or difference of Marian's needs to those of other children reflected both perspectives. From one perspective she saw

Marian as the same as other children, because she needs socializing and boundaries; 'in some ways she's a very normal little girl'. But, from a different perspective, there were issues about 'her ability to learn and to interact with the environment as it is set up'. Marian's mother described her views in these terms: 'I don't have orthodox ideas about education; I think it should be to suit the person; you have to have a variety of settings – you know, keep it child-focused.' When asked more specifically about whether Marian required teaching that was similar or different from others of her age, she replied: 'Well, she has a lot of TA [teaching assistant] support so a lot of her teaching is different because it's mediated through a TA'.

Teachers and teaching

Marian's mother described Marian's relationship with her teacher as 'a bit love - hate', but also said that Marian did not like her. Marian has expressed, for example, that her teacher had 'told me off today, I don't like it, she's always telling me off'. Her mother felt that Marian had been 'bullied horrendously by the reception teacher' and was pleased that Marian started to react against it. When I asked Marian about her relationship with her teacher she expressed ambiguous views. On the one hand she said: 'I kind of don't really . . . I like my teacher, but I like it when she helps me with my work . . . sometimes she does, but sometimes I don't really like it when she helps me.' On the other hand, she later said: 'I get on with her fine', and she confirmed this when asked if sometimes she did not get on well with her, she replied 'not really'. By contrast, her favourite teacher was the one who she described as being by the computer suite and this was because they both liked the colour orange.

Marian's mother felt very annoyed that she was not given the chance to get to know Marian's teaching assistant. She thought that 'by law they should be consulting with me and they don't'. When she had asked for the assistant to be at a meeting after school, she was told that the assistant finished work at 3pm. Marian's mother did not feel she knew much about the working relationship between the teacher and Marian's assistant. But she knew another teaching assistant at the school, a qualified teacher, who believed that the teaching assistants were not well treated generally at that school. Marian's mother also had doubts about the skills and knowledge of Marian's teaching assistant, explaining that 'I mean they're not getting any support. It's not their fault, but they're not getting any input.' She believed that the SEN coordinator did have some contact with the assistants, but the school's SEN coordinator was shared between schools.

Marian's mother also described a recent conversation with Marian about her assistant in which Marian said: 'I don't want any more TAs', which her mother interpreted as the TAs making her feel different. When her mother asked her why she did not want a TA, Marian explained: 'because I want to be the same as the other children'. When her mother then asked Marian 'If we took the TAs away would you be the same as the other children?', Marian said yes. Yet, during my talk with Marian, she talked about having 'help because I'm not very good at reading or writing'. Marian also talked in her interview about sometimes having arguments with her assistant.

For example, one was about: 'I don't need any help', to which the assistant said: 'you have to have help'. When this happens they leave the classroom and move to the computer suite.

From the advisory teacher's perspective, taking Marion's attention span into account would help her learning. From her observations this aspect was well managed as tasks were broken down into 'achievable chunks'. Using task planners would also support her learning so that she can actually see the steps that she needs to go through. Though Marian may present as quite articulate, she may not understand the language used, not just because of attention but also her ability to store it. So Marian requires quite simple concrete language to support her understanding. And, as the advisory teacher commented, this would affect her ongoing relationship with her peers as their language becomes more complex.

As mentioned above, her mother believed that precision teaching had helped Marian's learning. She also talked about a way of teaching Marian writing which had not been written into her IEP. On the conditions that make learning hard for Marian, her mother believed that because of her sensory processing issues, Marian became very distracted in a classroom with 30 children. So she felt that Marian needed a much smaller and quieter setting. She also believed that Marian needed a teacher 'with compassion, warmth and understanding'. She did not believe that her teacher needed 'some sort of textbook understanding of her condition, but I would be happy with a teacher who was just warm, sympathetic and who actually enjoyed Marian being in the class'.

When Marian was asked in her interview about what kind of teaching helps her learn, she talked about 'working independently'. She explained that 'sometimes I have a bit of support, but I sometimes get it, and get frustrated, really frustrated'. It was her teaching assistant, she said, who frustrated her . . . 'she does, she talks in a normal voice and says "What can you think of?" and it frustrates me and it makes my head . . . it makes my head up so I can't think. My head keeps spinning.'

School placement

When Marian was asked how she felt about her current school, her response seemed to be contradictory: 'It's fine, but not really.' When asked about the 'not really', she switched to talking about the school needing redecorating, pointing to the room that we were in. And when then asked how others treat her, she said 'I don't know . . . can we come back to it?'

The advisory teacher believed that the current school was suitable for Marian because there was a 'high level of support' and 'she was managed extremely well and she was experiencing good learning experiences'. She felt that without this level of support, it would be challenging for Marian. Whether Marian can manage in a secondary school setting will need to be reviewed. She added that a decision about whether something additional was required also depended on what provision was on offer in the local area and whether it would be better than current provision. When asked if Marian would do well in an ordinary school which had a specialist resource, the advisory teacher replied: 'I think that would be, it would be lovely wouldn't it?', recognizing that such provision was unavailable.

Marian's mother also believed that: 'ideally in some ways a unit attached to a mainstream would be good', recognizing that the only local unit or specialist resource was for children with visual impairments or autism. But she realized, following an educational psychologist report last year which mentioned the possibility of a special school for Marian, that this was an option. This coincided with her own thinking about a special school move at primary - secondary transfer. She explained that she was not shocked and did not 'do denial', while noting that 'it's a bit early really to be thinking . . . about transition in year 3 but I could see where the psychologist was coming from'. When asked if she had considered another primary school, she explained that the other one, a similar distance from where they lived, was even less suitable. The head teacher of that school has been known to tell parents who wanted a Statement for their children to go away. She concluded that: 'I've done a lot of homework; they're all basically a bit rubbish around here.' At this point in the conversation she mentioned that she had asked Marian if she would feel better 'in a school where all the children had to have TAs', to which Marian said yes. When Marion was asked in interview directly about going to another school she was aware that she might do so and that it would not be the secondary schools to which her friends would go.

As noted above, Marion's mother was not opposed to special schools because she felt that 'all schooling should be special'. She opposed a 'straightjacket approach to schooling' with 'one size fits all'. Some of the ethos she preferred for Marian was available to her outside school activities. Marian went to a local facility around the corner which she felt was very good for Marian because it is 'pretty unstructured . . . she also gets to play with children of different ages, so (there is) no pressure'. She will continue there until she is 11 years old.

Parental involvement

Marian's mother felt that the nursery school had been 'fantastic'. The problems started when Marian went into the reception class: 'the school have been pretty useless'. She believed that the issues were not just about teachers, but wider society. In her view teachers had 'specific issues because they're constantly being picked out to do a lot of things that in fact they're not remotely qualified to do, whether it's to do with disabled children or not'. It was 'through pot luck' that Marian 'has had three of the worst teachers since she's been there'. She described Marian's current teacher as 'monosyllabic' and 'ambivalent'.

Marian's mother had no feeling of being consulted or treated as a partner: 'They treat Marian as theirs to do with as they wish, but they do not see my involvement is actually a legal requirement. There's no reciprocity involved.' When asked about this, she said that: 'I've been told to my face basically "get lost".' In her experience she has found that professionals present themselves as highly qualified childcare professionals, which: 'I know full well they're not.' This was also evident in Marian's current school, where the teachers are 'lost'. She gave as an example a communication with the SEN coordinator who said to her: 'Oh, we need a prognosis of what to expect', to which Marian's mother replied: 'Nobody knows what to expect; the consultants don't know what to expect.' This was the SEN coordinator who was at the school only two days a week and, when asked for a meeting, Marian's mother was offered a date six weeks away, so: 'you feel you're being palmed off'.

Marian's mother felt unable to be on her own in a room with the SEN coordinator, partly because the coordinator did not do what was expected of her. At the last Statement meeting, Marian's mother explained there was a list of all the things that people were meant to do. One was about the SEN coordinator making a referral to the communication advisory team. When no support service letter arrived, Marian's mother phoned to find out what had happened. No referral letter had been sent by the SEN coordinator. So Marion's mother contacted the support service herself, explaining what had happened. Marian's mother explained that this was an example of her referral 'battles'. She knew that this team would be reluctant to respond to this referral because Marian did not fit the criteria for autistic spectrum. But, she found that this team were starting to recognize that: 'they can't just stick to these little categories'. She felt that they were getting better in responding to a referral. However, the advisory teacher, the one interviewed, who did respond to the referral, explained that it was only a one-off visit to assess Marian's needs, because Marian did not meet their referral criteria. The advisory teacher also explained that if a school did not meet the referral criteria, and it wanted the service, it could purchase their support, if they felt it was appropriate.

Marian's mother had not, in the past, considered making a complaint to the school, despite others urging her to do so. Though she had just printed out a complaints form, she was unsure about the point of complaining. She was concerned that these procedures did not 'have teeth', especially as 'they've taken away legal aid'. However, she knew that to go to Tribunal over her concerns, she would have to 'play the game . . . have your quiet chat with the teacher first, and then your quiet chat with the head teacher, and then your letter to governors'. She explained that: 'if you don't follow the procedure, you see, they chuck it out . . . I think, as a parent, you feel it's loaded against you'. However, Marian's mother did make a complaint to the school about the SEN coordinator, and this was the reason why the coordinator refused to be interviewed for this case study.

Marian's mother had been having some support from the local Information and Advisory Service for a couple of years, which had been mentioned to her by someone she knew. She was very positive about the support she had been receiving, but thought that 'they've not got enough teeth'. She was also a member of a few networks and groups, such as the Child Brain Injury Trust. She found the networks useful, as she explained: 'because we can compare levels of rubbishness in our lives and realize it's not personal'.

Social interaction

Marian described that she was going to visit her father the coming weekend to stay for two nights and visit her grandmother, something she looked forward to. When talking about her mother she mentioned that she could not sleep in her own room, so she slept with her mother. Marian's mother described Marian's behaviour at home as sometimes 'rude and challenging'. Her older brother tends to become irritated by Marian's behaviour because, as her mother explained, they have different personalities. She was 'more of a live wire than her brother'.

Marian talked about two friends in her interview, who she plays with at school on most days. She said they all 'loved One Direction'. She explained that she knew one of the girls from when she was at nursery school. She did talk about them having some disagreements, but could say nothing more about what they were about. She also said that she could not go to this girl's house because 'her wall is getting redecorated'. Marian's mother described Marian as wishing to have more social contact with peers than she has, both inside and outside school. Marian was also described as feeling that children avoid her, something she does not fully understand, according to her mother, and it is something that can upset her.

Future

Marian's mother felt that Marian could 'have a good life', explaining that: 'I don't see that any of the problems that she has should stop her from doing anything that she wants to do', because she has seen others do it. This comes from her experience of working with disabled people who had lived full lives; 'they've done it, and I know that I can do that for her'.

Marian was not able to talk about any future worries in her interview. For the advisory teacher, her concerns were about Marian being able to access learning in secondary school as the language becomes far more complex. Marian's mother's fears were about 'a continuation of what I have now . . . that I'm going to have to go and do something dramatic' in terms of taking her out of mainstream school. Were this to happen she might consider some 'alternative education' provision, but this was financially costly. In the longer term she considered the need for some continuing support post-school, but this was hard to contemplate.

Marian's mother described her relationship with Marian: 'I'm now seeing that I may have to be her carer in the long term. But I'm aware of that, so I'm looking at it more in a holistic way that in some ways what we need is a school community . . . where (she) can develop to the best of her potential in a caring environment and where I'm supported appropriately as a parent carer. That's what I hope for.' So, she wanted to find 'a school that is warm and compassionate, that is more geared towards Marian's needs, but also emotionally, not just academically. Whether that is a state school, whether it's a mainstream or a special I don't know – I'm flexible. That's my hope.' When Marian talked in her interview about her future she talked about a new house and garden as well as a school away from her current one, referring to the urban school she talked about previously.

3

Sharon

Parents: 'Try making it easier on the families, stretch your understanding as far as you can go when dealing with a child that's got special needs.'

'Parents are learning as we're going along. The parents' point of view really needs to be informed (by others), but in a respectful manner . . . so just be fully aware of what's going on. Listen to the parents.'

Background information

Sharon, 10 years old, lives with her parents and her older sister, 12 years old, and younger brother, 5 years old, in a small county town. She goes to a special school for children with complex learning difficulties after being at a primary school till she was 9 years old. Her parents were interviewed at home and her class teacher was interviewed outside school. Sharon was observed in a lesson for over an hour and interacted with me one-to-one alongside and mediated by her teacher.

Identification

Strengths and difficulties

Sharon's father described her as happy, sociable and very bubbly. Her teacher described her as very 'smiley'. Her father felt that she was getting to 'know her own mind' a little. By this he meant that she was starting to have a 'point of view on things'.

Her mother felt she was progressing 'really nicely'. Speech was an area where this was evident. Her mother explained that when Sharon was younger she had a tracheotomy operation because her throat was small and they wanted to make it larger. This was at the time that she was starting to make baby noises, which meant that it took time for her to start making baby noises again. Her talking has progressed since then and her speech is a 'lot clearer'. Sharon wears hearing aids, or, as her mother said, is supposed to, but she pulls them out as they seem to annoy her.

Despite this, Sharon was described as being able to remember songs: 'she's got a very good ear for music . . . she remembers the melody easily'.

Sharon also has mobility difficulties and is doubly incontinent. Her teacher talked about her movement as being very restricted so when given a choice, she prefers to be sedentary. However, the staff do not let this happen too often; 'we get her up and about moving'. Her teacher described a stiffness across one side of her body, but that her general gross and fine motor movements were also quite limited. Recently she has learned to raise her hands up above her head. When I visited her at school, she walked to the entrance with her teacher to meet me with enthusiasm. Her father described how she has managed to walk from her house to the centre of town and back, but it took several hours to do this. Usually they take a wheelchair for this distance. She can manage shorter walks of about half a mile; beyond that she experiences problems.

Sharon had a stroke when she was about 15-months-old leaving her with a palsy on her left side (paralysis with some involuntary tremors). Initially she lost all the movement down her left-hand side, and gradually, as her mother explained, through physiotherapy and everything else most of it was restored. Sharon continues with the physiotherapy because if she stops the palsy might set in again. Her father described this therapy as one of her physical needs.

Sharon was diagnosed with Down Syndrome shortly after her birth and also has an commonly associated heart condition. This is known as atrioventricular septal defect (AVSD), which was diagnosed before birth in a pre-natal scan, a condition her father called 'a hole in the heart'. For this she had a heart operation when she was about 12-months-old. Her mother explained how when one issue becomes reduced 'another one pops up'. More recently, Sharon has developed a stutter; her mother described this as her still getting the 'words out so, it isn't that bad, but they're keeping an eye on it'.

Her teacher described how Sharon 'loves to play, she loves to act, she loves to interact, especially with adults'. Her interactions tend to be non-verbal, with much movement and smiling; 'she's very funny and she likes to make you smile and she likes to be made to smile'. She tends not to interact much with other children, partly because in her teacher's view she is in a 'tough class' with other children with behavioural needs. She seeks out Play-Doh and is often drawing and writing: 'at the moment the two are very much the same thing for her'.

Her teacher described how, to understand her, you need to know the words she uses to represent what she's communicating. She is very capable of supporting her speech with Makaton signs, so everyone at school uses signing with her. This involves using signs with verbal communication and they are building up a repertoire of signs with her. She works with about 50 signs to express herself. Her ability to understand is at a higher level, though this is mostly at a two keyword level in a routine situation. Her mother is currently learning to use Makaton too.

Her teacher also described her attainment level in numeracy and literacy as at P5, working towards P6 (P scales are the national framework for attainment for pupils with learning difficulties and go from P1 to P8). In numeracy she is working at her number sense and in literacy she is recognizing words by reading them in specific contexts.

Sharon had learned recently to run and get around the playground at school, something the staff were very proud of her achieving. Her teacher saw this as arising from the fitness work they had been doing with her. This had resulted in 'raising her self-esteem' and her abilities too. Her teacher described how when they went on a trip in which they walked a mile and a half, Sharon 'walked almost the entire mile and a half and ran some of it'.

Initial diagnosis, labels and impact

Sharon's parents were told soon after her birth that they were doing some tests as she had a palmar crease on her hand. Her father thought that they were introducing the Down Syndrome diagnosis to them gently.

Sharon's parents recognized that her having Down Syndrome meant that she had special educational needs. Her mother also talked about 'global developmental delay', what her father described as 'mentally she's younger' and her having 'complex needs as well as the Down Syndrome'. Sharon's teacher described her class as one for children with profound and multiple learning difficulties (PMLD)/severe learning difficulties (SLD), so she said that these descriptors would be relevant to Sharon.

Sharon's condition had the effect on the family of 'a massive, a total change of lifestyle', in her father's words. They had been living outside the UK and so they decided that with the associated medical problems they would stay in the UK. One implication was the involvement of many different professionals – occupational therapists, speech and language therapists, physiotherapists, ophthalmologists, audiologists and cardiologists. For her father, who did the driving, this involved long car journeys to appointments, which he described as 'a full-time job'. There was constant stress for them. Sharon's mother remembered when Sharon had kidney failure aged 4 and was in hospital, that a nurse suggested that they see a psychiatrist to 'talk over how you're feeling because in the past two years you've been through such a lot'. However, more recently, as her father explained, there had been no critical situations, 'it's just regular keeping going with everything that we need to keep going with'.

When reflecting on whether there were any positive aspects of what they had experienced, Sharon's mother thought that they had become more patient. Also, the grandparents had become more involved and supportive of their family. The grandparents on the father's side had moved closer to where they now lived to be more supportive. Sharon's parents described how the experience gives you a different view on life. They described how they 'were pretty understanding and open-minded about a lot of things before Sharon was born, so we were quite accepting very quickly . . . but not a true understanding of what really happens'. This was clear to them with every little step that Sharon took. Other people around them also were aware too of how long it took for her to reach certain milestones: 'it was a massive thing', whereas others see child development as normal. Sharon's teacher saw the impact of Sharon's condition as massive for her family.

Sharon's father described how they were aware of the possible impact on Sharon's older sister and younger brother. So they had made an effort to minimize this as much as possible. Her older sister had spent much time travelling to the hospital with them when Sharon was in hospital, though at that time she was 18-months-old.

She would spend some afternoons or playtimes with Sharon and was protective of her at school. But when she was at school with Sharon, she was known as Sharon's sister, so she 'never had her own identity'. Her mother thought that her older daughter felt a little irritated with this and was pleased to move to secondary school without Sharon, and so 'have her own identity'. As regards how Sharon reacted to her difficulties, her parents talked about her feeling frustrated sometimes – for example, when trying to tell you something and you do not get what she means.

Statement/Plan

Sharon has had a Statement since she was 3 years old. It appeared that her parents had not yet been told when Sharon would have her Statement transferred into an EHC Plan. They were also not too familiar with the details of the new Plans.

The parents described a major change in how they experienced the annual review of the Statement from Sharon's previous primary school and now at her special school. As her father explained, annual reviews were a 'battle, you had to brace yourself' for. Her mother said that the battle was with the head teacher who interpreted the Statement from their own point of view rather than Sharon's perspective. By contrast, the annual review at Sharon's special school was 'amazing . . . everyone who is involved with Sharon, therapists and teachers and everyone that works with her comes together'.

Sharon's parents believed that the legal protection of the Statement/Plan could be useful when a child's needs change, to ensure that these changed needs are met. Her mother gave as an example, when a child needs to have a full-time rather than a part-time teaching assistant. However, they did not answer the question about whether parents could try to enforce the contents of the Statement, perhaps because their own experience was that they struggled to have Sharon's Statement interpreted in the primary school as they expected. Her mother mentioned that she had advised other parents about ways in which they could 'get what they want for their children'.

For Sharon's father, the new EHC Plans made good sense. He thought that Sharon was a good example of someone for whom it would be suitable, as it would bring together health and educational services in identifying her needs. One of his hopes for the new system was that it would enable parents to have second medical opinions. He described how they had some really 'good medical care, and we've had some really poor medical care'. However, Sharon ended up with kidney failure, because someone had failed to diagnose it properly. Person-centred planning approaches were used in formulating plans in the special school and this was about to happen for Sharon in the upcoming EHC planning; but this had not been communicated clearly to the parents.

Learning: what and how

Past and present provision

When Sharon was at pre-school, one which was not connected to the primary school she later attended, she had one-to-one support from a teaching assistant. Her parents found that the teachers, other parents and children were very accepting of Sharon. When Sharon went to the primary school, adaptations were made for her; they put in handrails and lowered steps. There was a plan which set out how they were going to include Sharon, but this was 'in theory, they talked the right words', but Sharon spent most of the time with her teaching assistant. The responsibility, as her mother explained, was put on to her teaching assistant. Sharon's mother explained how the head teacher would tell the assistant that Sharon was her responsibility.

Sharon's father described how, over time, the assistant began to tell them: 'you know, to be honest, this idea of inclusion isn't really working because I'm sort of working more one-on-one with Sharon, apart from the rest of the group'. While Sharon was in reception year there was much general play and she fitted into the class activities. But in the subsequent years there was less visual input for her, and her understanding, according to her father, did not progress compared to her peers. So Sharon's parents decided that it would best for Sharon to go back two years to the reception class, something which also involved the educational psychologist's agreement. However, it then became apparent that the local authority policy was that children go back only one year. This then became an issue between Sharon's parents and the school. Sharon' s mother contacted the Down Syndrome Association (DSA) which advised her that if the psychologist had advised the move to reception, this was what mattered. The DSA also told her mother that the authority could only advise; it was for the head teacher to make the decision. But the head teacher told them that she did not 'want to go into battle with the authority. Sharon's parents also considered going to the Independent Panel for Special Education Advice (IPSEA) for them to advise on what they could do. But they did not have to do this because the head teacher finally backed down and agreed that Sharon could stay in the reception class, though not register as in that class, and that she would go to secondary school when 11 years old.

When Sharon finally went to the local special school, at 8 years old, after previously doing sessions there part time, her parents felt able to relax after the 'constant fight to get anything for her'. They felt that the special school was well organized and that there were the therapists that she needed in the school itself. This meant that appointments took place during school timetable. Sharon's mother, when reflecting about the primary school, believed that it was 'very officious and not centred around the child, it's centred around the teachers and the classroom setting'. This summed up her views about how statementing was interpreted in the ordinary compared to the special school. Her parents were very satisfied because they felt that Sharon had progressed a lot, with the curriculum being 'based around her'. They gave, as an example, if she needs a little bit more physiotherapy on her leg, part of her curriculum would be to take a step up to the office so she could climb up stairs or go on a little walk. They also talked about the language and communication club that supported Sharon's communication skills. The school had also introduced a one-page profile that was used to indicate to those working with Sharon what they needed to know about her.

Sharon's teacher explained that she was in a class of seven children, a year 5–6 class, with five-and-a-half adults – what she called, 'high need'. Only one child was approaching reading and writing; the others were at a 'very emergent stage of beginning to control pencils, beginning to understand what a book is about'. The person-centred nature of Sharon's curriculum programme meant that it was structured around her needs, with different balances to the programmes for others in the class. For some in the class, maths and English is less important compared to social-emotional learning, while for Sharon she has a focus on English, maths and science, but also on physiotherapy and a programme called Fun Fit. This was a programme used to involve Sharon in core gross skills for children around the ages of 3- to 4-years old – for example, lifting her arms and stretching. In addition, there is a lot of outdoor learning in the forest school, and social learning, through activities like signing and music. The general group work also aims to build attention and memory. However, as her teacher explained, there was not a specific focus on history and geography: 'it's more about the immediate and the experiential, building that experiential back into the communication and the interaction'. The occupational therapist (OT), also comes into class, perhaps for other children, but the activities that they organize might involve Sharon too.

Goals, engagement and progress in learning

Termly goals are set with her parents that focus on her daily living skills, such as toileting. There were also goals about physical orientation, mobility and gross motor skills – moving, running, walking. In addition, there are goals about communication and interaction, such as, moving from two keywords to three keywords. These, and other goals, are written in a plan of about six pages.

Sharon's parents discussed how the school communicated with them about her progress. They would be shown, for example, what Sharon was communicating after one term using a scale that indicated the progress made. The speech therapist would, for example, show Sharon's achievements using bar charts to show her use of two- or three-word sentences. As her mother explained, this was 'fantastic', as the method showed where Sharon was managing and where not, and the next steps for her learning. For example, the speech and language therapist informed them that Sharon was able to tell a story using connectives.

Sharon's teacher explained how the action plan was co-written with her parents, with Sharon herself present and taking part, using a person-centred approach. For Sharon, this involved using symbols to communicate with her about how the others involved saw her. To find out Sharon's perspectives, various sources – such as pictures, symbols or videos – were used to communicate what she has been doing and achieved.

Sharon's parents realized that what she needed to learn was very different from their older daughter because the 'level of understanding makes a very big difference'. They still thought that Sharon needed to learn numeracy and literacy, but at a different level. Her father explained their thinking when saying that 'we focused so long on her health that we've always said "As long as Sharon stays well and is happy then that's sort of like a baseline. And then anything else she achieves on top of that for us is great."' He went on to explain that 'when you're looking ahead, when she's a late teenager and in her 20's . . . I'm not sure what level she will achieve, what level of independence and understanding'.

Sharon's teacher had a slightly different perspective about what programme Sharon needed, which was neither the National Curriculum nor a specialist curriculum; 'you can choose very specifically to look at capturing the interests of the children in your class and moving them forward . . . it's person-centred'. She saw the teaching as involving 'one-to-one in very short bursts for the children so that they're able to kind of engage with something that's probably similar to a foundation stage provision'.

Sharon's parents thought that it was important that she learned a basic level of literacy and numeracy, but also that social and life skills are really important. Her father said that 'I'm always pleased when I go in and speak to them; I never come away disappointed.' Her mother added that 'if there was something that we specifically weren't happy about at that school, and we spoke to someone about it, they would put something in place for us'. They both expressed their confidence in the school. By contrast, her teacher believed that there was a gap in Sharon's social interaction; she needed girls in her class.

Sharon was observed while she was interacting with a song-based video cartoon about removing animals from a set of them while singing an accompanying song. She swayed her head to the music and copied the teacher's movements, while smiling to the music. The task was to identify the number of frogs after one had been removed, which she did correctly, and was praised by her teacher. They continued this for about 35 minutes, when her teacher said that she was getting tired and they stopped.

Teachers and teaching assistants

Sharon's mother explained that Sharon's teacher had been teaching her for six months, before which she had had another teacher who had now retired. Sharon had come to like her new teacher and they got on very well, according to her mother, but next year Sharon moved on to another teacher, representing a move to secondary school level.

Sharon' s teacher was trained as a primary schoolteacher, but prior to that had experience working as a senior teaching assistant. She said that she saw her current teaching as more similar to the assistant work than her primary class teaching. This was in terms of the one-to-one work, building a relationship with the child: 'I think it's entirely different to the mainstream.' She also believed that she drew on everything she had learned in terms of pedagogical skills. She explained that her main motivation for working in this setting was to have opportunities not available to primary teachers to 'really focus on the children instead of setting up groups'. Mainstream teaching was difficult for her because there were few opportunities to 'recognize them (the children) as individuals and as human beings and what they really want and need'.

Sharon's teacher also discussed the training within the special school that supported her teaching – for example, reducing the spoken language used with children to meet their needs. Her main sources of professional learning came from the communications team. External professional learning opportunities were limited due to restrictions on funding which left a 'big gap'.

The assistants were designated as key workers for specific children, though they did also work with other children from time to time. The organization of working was that the teacher focuses on the core subjects with the children while the assistants tend to focus on the therapy activities. They all meet together once week to review and plan, but for only 40 minutes. So they tend to discuss general issues, with specifics being communicated by written notes or 'snatched conversations' at other times. In-service training for assistants is done in-school, mainly by the communications team.

What helps/hinders learning

Sharon's mother considered Sharon to be a 'very visual person', so activities and information needed to be presented visually rather than verbally – for example, using little charts to communicate in addition to Makaton signs. Sharon's teacher agreed with this, but also said that 'doing' is very important for her. She added that she did not believe that the activity necessarily needs to be a doing activity, but 'she needs to be moving in order to do the activity'. Music does not, in her view, cause the learning, but 'creates the engagement'. Auditory processing was something with which she has 'struggled'. This meant that it was important for her to have the time to process and for adults to wait until she knows what it is she is expected to do.

Placement

Sharon moved to the special school two years ago in year 4, after having been to some sessions three mornings a week in year 3 at the special school. This was for hydrotherapy, numeracy and speech and language therapy, which she attended with her teaching assistant from the primary school.

The parent's decision about the move was very much influenced by the teaching assistant who had supported Sharon throughout her primary school. Sharon's assistant felt a lack of support from the head teacher about making adaptations for Sharon. There was a close relationship between her and Sharon's parents. As Sharon's father explained, there was a 'list a mile long about her grievances because she dealt with it on a daily basis. She did her best to sort of keep us involved, but not sort of burden us with it as well.' Her father described the assistant as always giving '110%'. He described her as 'very able and independent minded' and believed that other assistants would have sided with the head teacher. How this assistant dealt with Sharon's nipping behaviour was given as an example. She would ask what was the reason for this behaviour, and once she had an answer would 'put something into place to stop it from happening'. For her parents, the final factor that influenced their decision to go for a special school was that her teaching assistant was leaving. Sharon's father mentioned that the special school was 'always at the back of our minds', and there was the agreement that Sharon would move from the primary school at secondary age. They realized that she might not go to a secondary school at 11, but, 'it came to a head a lot quicker because the assistant was leaving'.

Sharon's teacher believed that Sharon would do well in an ordinary primary school with a specialist setting or unit for the first years of primary school, because this would provide her with social opportunities. She did not think that being with children with behaviour difficulties, as at present, suited her because she needed to be nurtured in a small group setting. However, she did also think that as Sharon grows older, and given the gap between her and an average 10-year-old in year 5, a special school is 'probably a better place for her'. She felt that 'the danger in mainstream is always that children don't access teachers, that they're isolated with teaching assistants, and we see a lot of children come in at year 7 who have spent a good few years in a cupboard with a teaching assistant learning one-to-one'. She concluded by saying that she could not 'imagine her managing in an ordinary year 5 class, partly because she would be doing work which is so very different, and to be included within a classroom I think would be incredibly challenging'.

Sharon's parents believed now that there should be special schools, though they recognized that, before having Sharon, they thought that 'all schools should be fully inclusive'. As her father explained: 'mainstream schools should just do their best to cater for everyone'. But, he went on: 'the reality of it is she just gets so much more attention to her specific requirements' at the special school. However, he did also believe that 'there should be . . . a bit more bridging between the two'. For Sharon's mother, 'inclusion doesn't work a lot because in mainstream school there are 30 children in the classroom and sometimes an assistant is just a classroom assistant for everyone and not specifically for one child'. Sharon's teacher also explained how she was very critical several years ago about special schools. But her experience of a nurture group in a primary school made her see how children with various kinds of special educational needs can be enabled to 'move forward and be valued as individuals for what they really need'. In her experience these children were able to experience 'the teaching that they really needed', and then in the afternoon 'they would be included in the wider primary school, they had opportunities for inclusion at playtimes with adult support. And I think in some ways that is ideal, particularly when they're younger.' But, in her experience, this special school enables Sharon 'to be happy, to be healthy and safe and . . . develop at the very best rate that she possibly can'.

Parental involvement

Sharon's mother was very satisfied with her relationship with Sharon's current school staff. She visits the school regularly, but her father was less involved than when Sharon was at the primary school, as he used to do the driving. Now the school bus picks her up for school outside their home. Sharon's teacher talked about the termly home-school agreement and target-setting process with parents. Connections are kept up with home, she explained, when they visit the school, by occasional phone calls and the home-school book that goes between her and the parents daily. She also felt that Sharon's parents were satisfied. She did, however, think that the parents were anxious about Sharon being in a special school and 'the experiences that she will have of other children as a result of . . . being in special school'. She gave, as an example, how when she tells Sharon's mother about the positive things Sharon has done, that her mother seems to be relieved.

Since the disagreements with the head teacher at the primary school, Sharon's parents had not experienced any similar disagreements with professionals. This was confirmed by Sharon's class teacher. Her parents had some contact with the Down Syndrome Association, but had no links with local support groups. As her parents explained, they had not felt the need, partly because with their other two children, they tend to do things as a family.

Social interaction

Sharon's mother discussed how Sharon had no contact with children who live locally. As her father mentioned, she does not have other 10-year-olds coming over to play, because she needs someone with her at all times. But, he felt that it 'could be more of a problem if we allowed it to be'. Despite this, she has been invited to a party of someone from her special school, and she has been on outings. Her mother described how this was a common experience for other parents whose children have SEN. This is where her having siblings was fortunate as 'she does get about through her siblings'. But her mother recognized that when Sharon was at primary school she was invited to more parties than since she has been at special school.

Her social relationships at school have varied between the primary and special schools. When in the reception class at the primary school the younger children did not have any spatial awareness about the effect of them being right up close to her. This was when Sharon went through a period of nipping other children because she could not voice her irritation with them being in her face. At the special school, Sharon was described by her teacher as having 'really good relationships with all the children', reflecting that 'everybody just thinks the world of her because she's got such a beautiful smile and she so wants to talk to you'. But her teacher felt that Sharon needed to be less adult dependent. There was a general tendency for the children not to engage independently with each other, something the staff were working on. Sharon had learned to use the phrase 'I want . . .' and recently had started to use it with reference to specific people; she would say 'I want play Sally', where Sally is the teaching assistant. This is beginning to be transferred to children now. Sharon also had some social interaction with children from a nearby primary school at the forest school, which was a shared space between the schools. Here the children would learn to mix with what her teacher called 'neuro-typical' children. The special school staff had taught some of the primary children how to sign with the special school children.

Sharon was described by her parents as getting on better with her siblings because she had 'more of an understanding about things now'. Her older sister enjoyed different activities to Sharon, but her younger brother, being five, was keen to play with Sharon. Her parents described how Sharon has grown up in a 'normal family situation'; as her father said, 'it's our normal situation; it has been for ten years'.

Future

Sharon's mother found it hard to look forward to the future: 'I just like to take each day as it comes because it scares me quite a bit.' She talked about an experience she had had in town when she saw a woman in her twenties with Down Syndrome walking on the other side of the road. She had similar hair colour to Sharon and she 'saw for an instant what Sharon would look like in the future'. She noticed how others responded to this woman; giving her 'a strange look and avoided her'. She wanted to think that this would not happen to Sharon, but recognized that 'it probably will. We can't protect her.' Sharon's teacher also had worries about Sharon's future which were about Sharon being very passive and doing very little. She also had a 'political social fear that when she becomes an adult there won't be the care and the support there within our society that she needs'.

Sharon's father shared a similar anxiety about her future. He said that he 'thinks about it all the time'. But, when he thinks that she is now 10 years old and that for another ten years she will continue at the special school, he was very thankful; 'being at the special school actually is quite an important part of having some confidence about the future'. He was unsure what these years will involve; 'whether it's a sort of gradual move to the learning independent life skills'. Sharon's mother wanted to think that 'she would be able to maybe hold down a little job, but she would be independent'. Her father agreed with this but qualified his views by talking about achieving these goals with support. He wondered what it would have been like if she had continued at the primary school, concluding that 'we would have been in a really tricky situation yet again at secondary transfer, where now it just seems to be settled'.

4

Ben

Mother: 'I would say, just go with your gut feeling about what's right for your child . . . but you don't want your child in any school that says it doesn't want your child . . . I would say to teachers, 'Get out of your comfort zone, you know, use your brain, and find out about somebody who's a bit . . .'

Teacher: 'You don't look at the label, you look at the need. And you look at where they are developmentally, absolutely; he's not 12 – developmentally he's 18 months. You use what you know about children of that age to inform your plans for that child. If you wouldn't expect an 18-month-old child to sit on the carpet for 40 minutes, why would you expect him? If you wouldn't expect a child of that age to be able to give a reason for their behaviour, why would you expect him?'

Background information

Ben, 12 years old, lives with his parents in a city suburb. He has two sisters who are young adults. He has been at a local primary school and is about to go to a special school co-located with a secondary school at secondary transfer. His mother was interviewed at home and his SEN coordinator interviewed at school. Ben was observed for over an hour working with his teaching assistant in the library.

Identification

Strengths and difficulties

Ben's mother described him as a 'clever little boy' who was charming, affectionate and had a lovely personality, with a 'big bad sense of humour'. His main difficulty, as she described it, was communication. Despite this he could recognize and become very excited when he heard a foreign language, like French. She thought that he was 'really focused on sounds and words' and she linked this to his liking of poetry, music and songs. Ben was described as being able to learn some songs, by contrast to him not learning 'other stuff'. She described how she kept him entertained by song when he was young, long enough to eat a meal.

His mother described how he likes being outdoors, likes birdsong, sowing seeds and growing plants. Ben also likes the television which he watched by standing very close because of his vision. During the interview he watched the television most of the time, right up close to the screen. His mother explained that sometimes he stops looking at the pictures and just listens to the sound. She also believed that he understood 'more than he let's on, communicates or shows'. This comes out sometimes by what he says and does: 'we find him out because he gives it away every now and again'.

His mother and teacher described how he started to enjoy walking in the last two to three years. His mother talked about him not walking till he was 5 years old because of his very poor muscle tone and lax joints. So he can now go on a walk with his family, which his mother said has 'made a massive difference to him'. His teacher explained that at school he was still in nappies and does not notice or is not bothered when he is wet. The routine at school is that he is taken to the toilet every hour. He also needs to be fed at home. As his mother pointed out it, 'you can't starve him . . . and you would be the loser because you wouldn't get him to school on time, he'd have a terrible day at school'. His behaviour would deteriorate or he would not sleep if he did not have his meal. However, Ben does eat more at school; he was described as going in phases, sometimes interested in eating and at other times not. His teacher summarized his self-help skills as being at or below 'an 18-month-old level developmentally'.

Ben's visual impairments began when he was born without vision. At about ten weeks he had a cataract operation restoring short-sighted vision in one eye and long-sighted vision in the other. He functions by switching between his eyes and the squint he had has now been straightened out. But, as his mother explained, he still has a significant nystagmus and the professionals have had continuing difficulties in assessing his distance vision. She described how Ben uses his short-sighted eye for looking at books and sometimes sees more of the detail than she would have expected. He has never seen the world in focus, so she assumed that he does not expect things to be in focus. Ben has also resisted wearing glasses. As soon as he could get the glasses off, he refused them. At nursery school they even tried having all the children wearing glasses, to no avail. He does not tolerate eye exams and so has had to have a general anaesthetic to have a full eye examination. Even measuring his weight and height has been challenging. His mother also explained that he can become distressed and stay in a bad mood for quite a while. He was described as 'suddenly flipping' and 'you just don't know why'.

Ben's teacher summarized his learning and development as around P4–P5. When she first met him, when he was in the nursery school, he would sit staring at a light box; from that age he was very stimulated by the light. Since then he has made 'huge progress', moving from P1 to P5. He now responds to his teaching assistant and can follow a simple instruction, such as, 'Find the blue bear and put it in the yellow pot.' His teacher also described how Ben can give a word in response to a phonetically segmented word, so if he hears 'C-A-T', he can tell you it's 'cat'. This was something that he could not do two or three years ago.

He can also repeat phrases that he hears from the classroom, such as, 'be quiet' using them in the right context. So, his teacher concluded that he can now use some language with meaning, rather than in a random way. He was also learning some basic numeracy skills, such as reciting numbers. He is adept at using an iPad independently for cause-and-effect games, and uses a large touch-screen computer. When Ben was observed working with his assistant he said 'Marmite on toast', which was unrelated to what was going on. He could say 5 after 4 and could say 'five' when she pointed to a 5. He showed his understanding of spoken language by pointing on request to the 'teddy with the ball' in a picture. Though he struggled with some sorting tasks – e.g. sorting cars, aeroplanes etc. into going on the road or going in the sky - he was able to sort things into red and green objects.

Causes and impact

Ben's mother believed that his main diagnosis of Down Syndrome was relatively 'minor compared with a lot of the other stuff that's gone on for him'. She also wondered if he had autistic spectrum disorder, but they have not gone for a diagnosis. She did also wonder if Ben's behaviour in this respect might be linked to his cousin who had autism, and whether there was a family link. Ben's teacher also mentioned autism and explained that his parents had not used this diagnostic route because the benefits were unclear.

According to his mother, Ben's main special educational need was about his inability to communicate what he thinks and feels and a growing issue about impulse control. She described how he sometimes 'gets frustrated and violent'. This often occurs when he wants her to do something or wants something and cannot make his needs clear. This is when he 'flails around and hits out', something which has tended to increase recently. She also saw him as anxious, showing behaviour like 'hyperventilating, twitching and twisting his elbows and ankles'. She was upset by these behaviours and would like to relieve him more, but felt 'sorry that we can't do more'. His teacher described Ben in similar terms at school, becoming 'very grumpy, distressed and crying'. They often do not know what he is asking for, and though they can sometimes use distraction to bring him out of his mood, at other times he can be 'very dismissive'.

Ben's teacher said that she would describe him as having severe learning difficulties. She found this a difficult assessment to make, but that it was because he took so long to learn. She also linked this assessment to his self-help skills. She explained that if he was in a room with no adults, 'he wouldn't be able to get himself a drink, he wouldn't be able to get himself food'.

Ben's mother described the impact of Ben's difficulties by comparing Ben with his older sisters. She described how her husband and she had come to adopt an attitude of not worrying about the older daughters by telling them, 'do whatever you want to do that makes you happy and we will support you'. They felt a release from that kind of social pressure for Ben; the view that 'your child has got to do this, this and this'. She summed up her position as: 'you just have to let your kids be who they are'. By doing that she felt that they had made many 'good friends' through the Special Friends club that they would not have done otherwise. They had also done things that they had not done before: explaining that 'it breaks down a lot of barriers, a lot of ridiculous ingrained social snobbery, I mean all sorts of rubbish just goes out the window'. She talked about going next weekend to a caravan park for four days with this club. But, she admitted that they were 'obviously knackered' by Ben. His teacher wondered if Ben's parents were finding things more difficult at home as Ben was getting older and stronger and perhaps more aggressive. She knew that someone had put his parents in contact with an organization that could offer some respite care.

Labels and how others respond

Ben's mother explained that she did not 'really mind what anyone says' about Ben. She recognized that his main diagnosis was Down Syndrome and she was now beginning to feel that she might initiate some investigations related to him having autism. She seemed to experience some tension about the significance of him having an autism diagnosis; 'Oh well, what the hell, what does it matter?' Up till then she did not see the point of having a diagnosis, as 'it doesn't help us because he really has the maximum learning support he can get, it wasn't going to do anything for him, and he doesn't like those kinds of investigations'. But, on the other hand, she saw some benefits in being able to say to some people: 'And yes he does have an autistic spectrum disorder so please don't expect him to comply with your regulations.' For her it was useful to be able to say, 'he's not going to do that . . . it's not because he's totally disobedient and I'm a failure as a parent, it's because . . .'. So, perhaps when Ben is 19–25 she would go for the diagnosis as it would 'give me a lot of access to stuff when he's older'.

His mother described how some people stare at Ben, but in the community in which they live everyone knows him. Some of the children in the vicinity went to the same nursery as him or go to the same primary school, so they are accepting and 'really supportive' of him. She described when the children in year 3 wanted to ask her questions about Ben. So Ben was taken out of the class and they wanted to know why he was short and why he did not talk. She said to them that 'maybe they can get him to talk' and overall she felt it was a 'good exchange'. Ben's teacher also described how Ben experienced no negative reactions from his peers. She thought this was because he has been with the same peer group from reception year. Even if Ben makes a noise at assembly, for example, others have learned to ignore him. She also felt that the other children had learned much from Ben being around them, that 'we're all different, and that it's not all about getting your level 5's'.

His mother described how she has developed a 'thick skin'; 'so if people stare at him . . . small children really stare at him. I sometimes stare back at them so that they understand how it feels.' She also recounted an incident when she was doing a course and there was a young man with autism struggling to sit at the table. The woman sitting next to her said that she could not stand being near this young man.

Ben's mother said to her, 'but that's my little boy in ten years' time; and so she had a conversation with her and the woman revealed that she had not met anyone like him before. For Ben's mother this incident confirmed her belief that people need to know people like Ben and then 'they're not scared of them' and might be less likely to abuse them in later life. Ben's mother also remarked that disabled children seem 'incredibly sweet and cute', but people are terrified of disabled adults. Ben's mother also talked about other incidents relating to Ben and how she felt she needed to say to some people, 'tell me how you think your child has suffered by the presence of a child with additional needs in their class'.

Statement/Plan

Ben was issued with a Statement of SEN when he was at nursery school. A decision was taken recently to transfer his Statement into the new Education, Health and Care (EHC) Plan. The paperwork was done by the SEN coordinator, Ben's mother, an educational psychologist and someone from the visual impairment team, over many hours. However, it came back with a request that the outcomes for Ben be more specific. So they were still working on this transfer at the time of the interviews.

Ben's mother was positive about the new EHC Plan system because she saw the Statements as school-led, while there were other areas of support needed concerning health and social care. So she saw the EHC Plans as being very relevant to Ben's needs. But, she also felt that every child should have an individual educational plan, because 'one size doesn't fit all'. In her view every child could have a Statement/Plan, which for 'some would be complex and for others really simple'. But she realized that 'the system doesn't work like that . . . and you have to live in the world you live in rather than get really stroppy and be really idealistic 'cause you just haven't got the energy'. She also expressed her dissatisfaction with the 'game' that she had to play: 'you have to present the worst case scenario, and the minute it looks like anything is going well or anyone's making progress then they're like, "Oh well, you don't need so much help any more".' She then would have to explain that the progress made depended on the support, so it should not be withdrawn. So, she explained, 'you have to lie in your boots about stuff, it's a horrible process . . . you have to really plug away at stuff, you appeal against decisions, it's a massive hard work'.

Ben's mother saw the system as too bureaucratic and believed that it was for schools to say what they needed to help children with additional needs, they should not need to justify it in terms of detailed accounts of what children could not do. Ben's teacher also had doubts about the Statement (and the new EHC Plan) system being relevant to the current context. She explained that Statements were initially required to secure resources into schools, but now that funding was allocated to schools, primary schools could manage provision, through differentiation and bringing in specialist people when we needed advice. But, she believed that if she was a parent she 'wouldn't be confident that as the child moves into secondary school that they're going to get that provision'. In her experience, even children with Statements in secondary schools did not receive what they needed.

Ben's teacher was also impressed by the new EHC Plan system extending from birth to 25 years, but anticipated some issues over understanding the ECH Plan and confusion over the criteria to be used for issuing Plans. She also wondered if it will be more difficult to get an EHC Plan than a Statement as the threshold is going up.

Learning: what and how

Provision

Ben's mother was very positive about his primary school, 'they're really good, a very good head teacher and a really good management structure'. She described how when Ofsted inspected recently they were able to show with data how Ben had made progress. The school had been very flexible with Ben, letting him go back to the reception group to enable him to keep doing certain things.

Ben's teacher explained that they keep him in his class as much as they can, being with his peers during registration and for topic work. She described his teaching assistant as very skilled in adapting the topic work to suit his needs. For example, if the children were learning about planets, they would do light and dark and the moon and the sun, focusing on a part of the topic. She estimated that he spent about 40–45 per cent of the time in year 6, now that the others were working on the national tests (SATs). She described how Ben and his assistant have a working space where they go and focus on number rhymes and songs, counting, developing his speech and language. As these activities can be noisy, she explained, this was a reason for being out of the class. My observations of Ben were during one of these withdrawal sessions. He also joins the reception children for letters and sounds sometimes, which she noted have taken a long time for him to acquire. Though he is starting to know them, he does not apply them independently.

Ben's teacher also discussed external support for his learning from the visual impairment team, the speech and language therapists from one of the specialist settings and the educational psychologists. Overall, she did not see this support as consistent. In her view, his schoolteachers managed by 'looking at him developmentally'. That he had made progress, in her view, was 'only down to the dedication of his teaching assistant, her skill, and the appropriateness of his provision'.

Ben had attended a special school for children with severe learning difficulties for two days a week for extra physical education and music therapy for two years up till two years ago. This stopped when others in the group with him were moving on and there was no appropriate group for him to join. His teacher explained that after this happened she started to worry that the primary school did not have the same facilities as the special school – for example, the withdrawal areas, sensory rooms and soft play areas. But, as she explained, they did their best buying equipment and giving access to touch-screen computers and iPads.

Ben also took part in a choir after school, with the school paying for an assistant to support him there. He performed at the local concert hall with the choir, something which he really enjoyed doing. His teacher explained that he did not always sing along with the others; he might sing later, but it was 'something he loves to do'. His mother also described this concert as something Ben loved to be part of. She described Ben as 'passionate about music' but that he became 'hysterical' to the extent that she worried he would ruin it for others there. When she went to the toilet with him a woman approached her to say that 'he's making us enjoy it more'.

Learning goals: adapted and relevant

Ben's teacher discussed that he needed to develop a way of communicating his needs. He did use a few words but typically adults had to 'pre-empt what it is that he needs'. Though he can sometimes choose between two options he cannot answer an open question. She also believed that he needed to 'have some experience of being independent from his family'. What was relevant for him to learn was to 'know how to go to the local supermarket and buy some food, he needs to know how to get on a bus, he needs to know how to do his laundry, how to keep himself clean, and he needs to be doing that with other young people so that he doesn't feel different'.

Ben's mother agreed with his teacher's views about what was relevant for him. She was opposed to 'pressurizing children to get GCSEs'. These views connected with her beliefs about the need for a basic change to the education system which was 'informed by all sorts of dogma that people cling to' and 'people aren't flexible, they don't think flexibly'. She described how some people had been critical of Ben not being with his peer group, while she thought that 'he was fine going back to reception, he was having a lovely time'. From her perspective, 'a school should be a place where people go to find out what they want to find out and they should be surrounded by people who enable them to do so . . . and people should sit where they like, with whom they like, and no one should be educated in a tight little peer group'. But, for that, she realized that there would have to be 'a massive educational revolution'.

Teachers and teaching assistants

Ben's mother described how his class teachers have varied in their interest in and understanding of Ben's needs. Ben has had some teachers whose attitudes she summed up in terms of: 'Oh my goodness, that one is going to muck up my chart' and so 'never planned for him'. She gave as an example one male teacher who the teaching assistant 'eventually took aside to say, "You are just so messing this up; you need to start taking notice of Ben and you haven't included him."' By contrast, Ben's mother saw his assistant as 'fascinatedly interested in him'. She was seen as knowing where Ben is, what he was doing, and as planning more for Ben than most class teachers; though she did add that Ben's current teacher was very interested in him.

Ben's mother saw his teaching assistant as having skills in setting him 'quite high standards' and recognizing what Ben could understand since he had been using an iPad. While doing this she was very consistent, affectionate and supportive. Ben's mother was also impressed with how she could say 'no, you can do that by yourself' and keeping him 'motivated by praising him, but, praised him for doing the right thing'. Ben's assistant had started as a nursery nurse, and had worked at a special school before coming to the primary school where she had worked for 22 years. She had the usual teaching assistant training and had worked with advisory teachers and therapists in relation to Ben.

What helps/hinders learning

Ben's mother described how he learns by rote, especially if it rhymes and there is some rhythm; this is where song becomes an important way for him to learn. His assistant had for many years, for example, sung him a weather song at the start of the day. His teacher also mentioned that Ben responds very well to routines. However, his mother found it difficult to motivate him – for instance, once he has learned something he can use it for a while, but then loses interest. Feeding was an example where he has the capability to feed himself, when with a stranger and some food, but will not do so at home. Though Ben likes rewards, either as stars or food, he tends not to connect these to his actions. His mother also believed that being outdoors helped to focus him – for example, being with animals. Artificial lighting was also not conducive to him seeing well, nor high-pitched noise and aggressive tones which can upset him. His mother also explained how if he is 'told off' or witnesses a row this can upset him for a long time.

Placement

Next school

Ben was due to go after the summer vacation to a school some distance from his home. It is a special school located on the same campus as a secondary and primary school. His mother said that the main reason for them choosing this school was the head teacher having the 'right attitude'; she found him to be 'really warm and friendly'. She was also impressed by the physical environment, the 'high staff-to-child ratio', and 'the children were engaged with what was going on'.

She expected that he will be distressed to start off but eventually become used to it. She thought that the most difficult aspect will be no longer having a one-to-one support worker. She was expecting that he would go into a class of about six children, based more on abilities than age. She also wondered if this would 'give him a sense of himself, as until recently . . . every transaction is negotiated through somebody else'.

His mother talked about the issue of how Ben would get to this school. Though there is a bus which he could take, she thinks the journey will be too long. So, she will be negotiating to have him taken by taxi. That the school was not in their community was an issue for her husband and herself. Ideally they would have wanted him to go to a local secondary school which had a group of pupils working at his level. It was an academy where the head teacher had recently lost his job for being 'racist' and the school was in 'special measures'. So, she felt disappointed about this, which Ben's teacher also mentioned in her interview.

Ben's parents had also considered schools in other parts of the country which would mean that the family would have to move house. But in the end they felt that the family needed to be near their friends; as his mother explained, 'you're juggling his needs with our needs'. They had also considered other more local secondary schools, but although one school said that it would 'give it a go' with Ben, his mother felt that she did not want a school to just give it a go; she 'wanted to hear their strategy'.

Ben's teacher discussed how his parents were 'very keen that he should stay in mainstream as long as possible'. Despite several school visits she described them as being 'undecided because they really want him to stay in his community'. Ben's teacher believed that if Ben went to a local secondary school he would not be included; he would be in a 'separate class most of the time', given Ben's complex needs. She thought that the co-located special school where he was going was 'absolutely lovely'. She explained that Ben's parents liked it because 'there's the opportunity for him to be . . . in the mainstream for some lessons and for mainstream kids to come to the specialist setting'. But, as Ben's mother mentioned, sending him to the co-located special school was 'a major compromise . . . but we feel that this is our best option with things as they stand'. By contrast, his teacher felt the co-located special school was an ideal placement, 'where everyone could come together for assembly . . . where the children, for their lessons or their learning experiences, would go off to an appropriate space'. She recalled, when younger, thinking that closing special schools was 'really good'. But since then she has come to believe that 'there should be special schools' as 'for some children that's the only place where they're going to manage'.

Parental involvement

Ben's mother and teacher had very similar views about the positive relationship between parents and teachers. Ben's mother felt there was good communication between her and Ben's teacher through the home-school diary they exchanged and that she could contact the SEN coordinator at any time. She was also confident that his teachers had enabled Ben to progress in his learning, expressing this in terms of having 'to prove that they are giving him an education, otherwise the local authority would demand that he were moved to special school where he would be less expensive'. Ben's teacher recognized that teachers varied in their inclusive attitudes and that Ben's mother would express her views if she felt that a teacher was not inclusive enough.

By contrast, Ben's mother felt that the support services and relationships with these professionals was 'very patchy'. Her experience was of many changes in staff so that she had to explain the same background to each new professional. She described how she was often reluctant to meet new staff because she wondered what they had to offer. But one community paediatrician insisted on meeting her and did refer her on to a community nurse service which has been very useful. However, in her view, speech and language therapy overall at the primary school was 'really bad', despite having had some who were 'good'. She did see one of the benefits of the special school next year being more consistent therapy services.

Ben's parents had a couple of incidents of disagreement over Ben's provision, but these were eventually resolved. The first one was about keeping him back a year when in the nursery years. The authority wanted to move him on, but his mother threatened to go to Tribunal. The authority then backed down saying, as Ben's mother reported: 'Oh, we wouldn't like you to have to go through the trauma of a Tribunal.' As Ben's mother remarked, 'you do have to keep plugging away'. The other point of disagreement was over music therapy. When he had been at the special school part time he had experienced music therapy. Ben's parents wanted this to be continued at his primary school when he stopped going to the special school, but the authority said it was not in his Statement. In the end the school agreed to fund the music therapy, and only then was it written into his Statement. This was sustained by the school because most of the SEN funding came direct to the school.

Ben's mother described how they had become involved in a local Special Friends group for about five years. She was invited by another mother who had a child with developmental delay, and their experience has been really positive. She described it as a 'real laugh' and for some parents 'it's a complete lifeline'. She explained how some parents were not as thick-skinned as her and did not like taking their children out if they were not going to behave well. So, the group enabled them to go 'mob-handed'; they go and do things as group, such as go to the cinema together, and they do not have to worry about their children making a noise.

Social interaction

Ben's teacher described how he had developed an awareness of others – adults and children – which was significant progress since he first came to the school. At that stage he would 'not interact with adults or with peers, whereas now he recognizes adults that he knows'. He eats his lunch with the other children using a special chair, with an assistant to check that he does not choke. Other children were aware that they needed to avoid hurting him: 'they kind of just go around him'. His teacher felt that the other children were mostly 'very nurturing towards him and they will play with him in the playground'. Ben interacts sometimes with some of the other children with SEN, but there are some specific children with whom he has a relationship. His teacher talked about one boy who looked after Ben and a girl who 'totally dotes on him', but he was not that interested in her. His teacher concluded that Ben did not have any firm attachments to any particular child, but 'he will just join in'.

Ben's mother described how a girl in Ben's class came up to her recently and said, 'Do you know what? Our school is not going to be the same without Ben.' Some others had also asked where he was going to secondary school, which his mother felt expressed their concern for him. His mother also described Ben's relationship with his older sisters. Ben talks to them over the phone or using an app; she described him as 'loving them to bits'. She also felt that they 'adored him and that they will always look after him'.

Future

Ben's mother saw his immediate future in terms of his new special school. She envisaged that he might continue there till he was 19 or perhaps 25. She saw this as really positive as she worried about provision being tightly linked to an age cut-off – 'you're 18; you're an adult'.

Ben's mother's immediate concerns were about him missing his assistant – what she called 'the end of that relationship', though she knew that his assistant would be willing to offer respite if they applied for respite care. His mother also had fears about what will happen 'once he's out of formal education'; this was her 'main fear'. While he was in education he has somewhere to go every day 'that's going to stimulate and interest him, and there's enough going on around him that he's not bored and he can continue to learn new skills'. Her fear was that adult services were being 'slowly whittled away'.

Ben's teacher described her hopes for him as he transfers to the special school; that they will 'continue to build on the progress that he's made already'. She also felt these skills needed to be geared to his life skills so he could develop 'some degree of independence as a young man'. But her worries were about how far he can acquire these self-help skills, and she was afraid that he might become 'institutionalized'.

Despite her worries, Ben's mother did feel very fortunate that his grandmother had left enough money to provide for him: 'that's really lucky . . . not everyone, hardly anyone can do that'. She also worried about the 'burden' they have given her daughters. She described a large extended family which was very supportive and that that would make it easier. She had a niece who is a lawyer who will be trustee of Ben's trust. Though she felt they were not 'leaving everyone with onerous stuff to do', she still felt guilty. She also mentioned how she has told her daughters that they must 'use the money to make your lives easy'.

5

Steve

Mother: 'At the infants school "listen to what the parents say"'. The parents know when there's something wrong, whereas the teachers seemed to say "No there wasn't."'

Father: 'I think it is that determination just to stay focused on, if you feel your child is dyslexic, then see it right through to the end. Don't get fobbed off . . . that determination is what got us through to where we are with the boys now.'

'I think with the teaching . . . what a dyslexic needs is good for every child, particularly at primary stage. It's a little bit more preparation, a little bit more thought. But a lot of it is low cost – it's not expensive. So just bring that into general teaching and you're just going to stay with your dyslexics doing a little bit longer than you are with those who are not dyslexic. It is so sad to see a state system that is no different than when I went through it.'

Teacher: 'My starting point is to like and respect the students I teach, and get to know them and get to know what they're good at and where they need that help'.

Overview

Steve is 14 years old and goes with his non-identical twin brother to a private school which has a dyslexia centre. He is a weekly boarder at the school and goes home at weekends, where he lives with his parents and an older and young sister in a rural area. Steve and his teacher, who coordinates the dyslexia centre, were interviewed at school, and his parents at their home.

Identification of needs

Steve's teacher at the time of the interview described him as an intelligent student, probably in the average to high-average range cognitively with severe dyslexia.

He believed that at the heart of his difficulties was a very significant weakness with short-term auditory memory that affects particularly his reading and writing skills. Though Steve had progressed a lot with his basic literacy skills, they were still significantly below average at age 14. His maths was extremely weak, and he suggested that Steve had a phobia for maths. Steve's strengths were verbal, with him excelling at speaking and listening. He is very articulate when they do formal speaking and listening tasks in class. He was also described as 'very good practically' and doing well at science. Overall, he saw Steve as 'not a smooth curve – there's up and downs along the way'.

His parents described Steve in comparison with his twin brother Bob, who was also identified as having dyslexia, but did not want to take part in this study. His parents described Bob as less verbal and quite shy, compared to Steve who was seen as the opposite. Steve was described as the smaller and older of the twins and being 'all front . . . he liked to be the class clown – he's always been naughty since he started school'. Though both boys had problems initially at school, Steve was the one who was identified by the teacher. As his mother explained: 'he'd started off in reception and year 1 by being naughty because he couldn't cope with any sort of work at all; he was naughty and they were just labelling him as a naughty boy, rather than any other problem'. She then explained that three of their children – Steve, Bob and the younger daughter – had all been identified as having dyslexia to varying degrees. Steve's father then emphasized that their sons were 'clever' and that with the literacy difficulties this led to frustration. He described how Steve tried to keep up with his peers and find ways round his reading difficulties. For example, he used to count how long it took his peers to turn over the pages during quiet reading and he would do so at the same rate, so nobody would notice that he could not read. His father recalled his concerns that Steve 'did not read well enough when younger to get through life', though he felt that 'he has pulled up a lot in the last 18 months'. His mother confirmed what the teacher said about Steve's hating mathematics; 'he doesn't like the maths teacher either, which is not helping now'. Steve leaves the tasks to others if he can, such as times tables and telling the time. His parents also described Steve's approach to learning as losing interest and not following through. His father believed that Steve had a short attention span that was not related to his dyslexia. However, he was very good at sports, especially rugby, which Steve himself confirmed. Steve also described himself as a social person who was not shy. He also described how he struggled with English and maths and talked about having dyslexia.

Initial identification

Steve's mother described how they asked the school when he was in year 1 to get an educational psychologist involved. She recalled a brief meeting with a psychologist, but Steve and his brother then moved to another primary school where the teacher did not report any problems initially. But, by the end of the first term in December, she wanted an educational psychologist to become involved. Steve was given the Toe by Toe reading programme, which his mother felt helped a little.

His father explained that Steve 'got the dyslexia from me, so I was aware of what was coming, or what to look out for'. This gave them an insight into the problem before they started. So, rather than the school flagging a problem to them, they were identifying problems in advance, such as being slow with writing and not identifying public signs, while his understanding and use of language was good. By this stage Steve's teacher had recognized that he was finding ways to conceal his literacy difficulties, and she began to monitor his reading more closely. The initial assessments came back saying that Bob was more likely to have dyslexia because he had the speech problems. When the psychologist's report came it did not use the 'dyslexia' word. They then said: 'Look – can we have the word included if it is relevant?', to which they then called out a specialist teacher who gave more practical advice. But his parents still felt that they did not know how severe the dyslexia was.

For Steve's father this was very disappointing as the situation for Steve was like it was for him 30 years ago. During his interview Steve explained that his parents used to talk to him about his difficulties in English and maths, especially when he was at the local primary school, but, since going to the school with the dyslexia centre they discussed it less. It was at this point in the interview that he disclosed that when he started at his current school he was 'four years behind everybody in English'. For his parents and teacher dyslexia was a genetic condition passed on through families. While his teacher emphasized the key factor being short-term memory, for his parents the hereditary aspects were evident in his father and Steve's brother and sister all having some degree of dyslexia. For Steve, dyslexia was a 'tricky question', but he recognized that dyslexia was a 'mental something' in which learning did 'not go into the brain' like for 'ordinary people'.

Implications of diagnosis

Steve's teacher was divided in his views about whether identifying dyslexia made any difference to how to teach. On one hand, he felt that it 'makes no difference whatsoever . . . you have a child in front of you who has clearly got some difficulties, where they came from doesn't really matter, you know, my job is to do my best for him'. But, on the other hand, he then suggested that 'I think it can help the child in that they understand that it's not their fault, and I think that's quite important.' The memory difficulties were also seen to make a difference to the way he taught in various ways: 'the crux of the matter is that if he has difficulties with his memory, he has to be taught in memorable ways, and everything kind of flows out from that really . . . short, sharp activities, making sure he's engaged with his learning and it's interactive'.

From her perspective, Steve's mother felt that she had learned a lot about herself through 'the journey with the boys, which has been extremely interesting'. But, she also found it 'quite upsetting that the boys had got these problems because it is something, though not something that's life-threatening or anything, that will severely hold them back'. For both parents, the dyslexia label was necessary to get help, so it was something they really pushed for. Steve's father felt that the current public understanding of dyslexia was 'very primitive'. Dyslexia was, for him, not just struggling with spelling, but having a 'problem with the written world'. For Steve, not being 'good at English makes you better at other things, such as sports'. He explained this in terms of concentrating more on something like sport, if you are less concentrated on literacy.

Steve's teacher considered that Steve had now begun to accept his difficulties and 'realized that if he works hard, he can work around them'. He suggested that he would have given a different answer three or four years ago. At that time he felt that Steve 'had quite a chip on his shoulder', though he was over it now. This had not come about by 'any magic wand . . . it's been a long, hard struggle'. He thought that some children change as soon as they come to this school because they realize that there are others with these problems: 'that's a kind of liberation for them'. He believed that this happened to Steve to some extent, but that with him 'it has taken quite a long time because . . . well, for a start, he did not make fast progress to begin with; it's been real hard work'. However, he thought that, for Steve, there was a positive aspect to his difficulties, which was that 'he knows that if he shows some grit and determination he can get things done, he can work round things and can achieve things'. He believed that Steve has shown some determination. But his teacher also realized that 'no matter how much help we give him, he's still going to struggle to achieve what he is truly capable of because of the difficulties'.

For Steve, having dyslexia made him feel frustrated and 'down a little'. He described how, when others in class have written hundreds of words and he has only written 20, he would feel 'far behind everybody'. He explained that he would cope with this by just trying, if he wanted to do the writing, not thinking about others' opinions. But, Steve was confident that these difficulties had not affected him getting on with others.

Labels and disclosure

Steve's teacher explained that they use the term 'dyslexia' at the school because it was a friendly word. His view was that for someone like Steve, who is going to get labelled anyway, it is important to be labelled in a way that people understand and is positive. So they use the word 'dyslexic', not just for the student, but so everyone in the school knows that it is a very specific difficulty, which is associated with being 'bright' and their own range of strengths; 'it's not a negative word at all'. He explained that the students at the school did not like anything linked to the phrase 'learning difficulties', such as specific learning difficulties.

His mother felt that the local authority 'would do anything to avoid mentioning the word "dyslexia".' She felt that this was because they would then have to take responsibility. They were even reluctant to say how severe it was. They happened to find out when talking to a special needs teacher at the primary school who happened to hear the educational psychologist use the word 'severe' about the twins. For Steve, he felt that the term 'special educational need' did apply to him; he felt that the term 'dyslexia' was about a special educational need, which meant that somebody 'has got something just a bit different or struggles a bit'. But he did not think that dyslexia was a disability, which meant for him, what 'stops you from doing things that you want to do'. An example of a disability was, for him, someone born without a leg. Nor did Steve feel bothered about going to the dyslexia centre at school: 'everybody's really chilled about being dyslexic'. The reason he gave for this was that 'in this school quite a lot of people are dyslexic, so all their friends are dyslexic'. When asked how he felt about being described as having dyslexia, he said that 'I don't really mind it, I mean there's nothing I can exactly do.'

His teacher described Steve as open about having dyslexia and suggested that, if he was having trouble with something, 'he would tell whoever it was "I'm dyslexic. I need a bit more input here".' So he'd stand up for himself. However, his father mentioned that Steve would 'within the environment he's in, a dyslexic school, use the word 'dyslexia', but outside . . . he'll avoid putting pen to paper because they'll know where his troubles lie'.

Statement

His mother explained how, despite an assessment by the psychologist and some additional assistance in primary school, the gap in the literacy between Steve and his twin compared to others in the class was widening. When they went to speak with the special needs teacher, he suggested that they try for a Statement, saying 'you need a stick to be able to hit them with'. But, he did not expect that they would get what they eventually did. So they started the statutory assessment process in year 4 when Steve was just 9 years old, and eventually he and his twin brother got them by the end of that year. The original draft of the Statement stated that he would receive an additional 15 minutes for English and another 15 minutes for maths. They then had a meeting with the specialist dyslexia teacher, someone from Information and Advisory Service, and an educational psychologist. This psychologist, who was newly qualified, was very supportive of the twins, and she revealed that they were 'severely dyslexic'. Steve's parents felt that had it not been for this psychologist the process would have been even more stressful.

Steve's mother described the process as like a 'full-time job', keeping on top of the legislation and linking with organizations like the Independent Parental Special Education Advice (IPSEA) to make as strong an argument as possible. They had also arranged for the twins to be assessed by a private psychologist who gave some useful practical advice and indicated that Steve had a very severe form of dyslexia, using the Turner Scale. The authority initially wanted to arrange for a specialist teacher based some distance from the school to visit the school. This meant she would have only one hour available per visit to help the twins, at a cost of £600 per day. So, they requested, using the Freedom of Information legislation to find out about the cost details, but did not receive anything. But eventually, as Steve's father explained, he pestered the authority almost on a daily basis till they gave them the cost details. When they got these they realized that for 'that much cost we can actually send both of them to a specialist school and save you money . . . can we go down that route?' But they did realize that had they wanted the twins to go to one local specialist school for pupils with dyslexia they would have had a bigger fight with the authority. The one they had visited was more expensive than the ordinary fee-paying school with the dyslexia centre that the twins went to.

This is how the twins came to go to their current fee-paying school with a dyslexia centre, what their father called a 'hard struggle'. Steve's mother also explained that the authority is still looking to make savings. This was about whether they go daily to the school or board weekly. Initially the boarding was because the twins were too young to travel daily, but now they were older questions were asked about this at a recent Statement review. The current arrangement is for the twins to board four nights a week. As for transferring the Statement into an EHC Plan, they were initially told this would take place when the twins were 16, but now the process will start later in the current year. Steve's mother did not think the new Plans would be any different, but wondered whether this might make a difference at transfer to sixth form and beyond, given that Plans go up to the age of 25.

Learning: what and how

Education provision

Steve's teacher talked about the three-pronged approach they use at the school. The first is the dyslexia centre where he gets the specialist teaching and provision he needs to improve his English language skills, reading, writing, and speaking. The dyslexic students actually do their English lessons there as well as the dyslexia-specific work. The second one is a whole-school approach to the teaching of dyslexic students, with a handbook, which contains advice and principles backed up by in-service training, so staff know how to adapt their teaching. The third prong is about building the students' self confidence and self-esteem, which is seen as being at the heart of everything. He also explained that school progress and effort are rewarded equally with attainment, and in addition to the academic programme there are lots of clubs and activities. Steve is in a small class of about six students in the dyslexia centre, which his teacher believed was beneficial through the interaction Steve gets with others.

Steve's parents contrasted his current provision with the provision he had in his local primary school. They realized that others had praised the school as providing well for a girl with autism, but they felt that this did not make up for what was not available for their twins. Steve's mother also noted that there was more interest in dyslexia at the school now the special needs teacher's son had been having literacy difficulties. Part of what their new school had offered was the dyslexia centre – as Steve's mother said: 'they don't feel like they're the only ones as they did in the state school; they were quite relieved to come home and say "Oh, he's as bad as I am."'

Though Steve's father was positive about the school's provision he wondered about how dyslexia-friendly it was in practice. He also wondered how up to date they were in using technology and up-to-date methods. Steve's mother was aware of the kind of provision used – for example, using foreign language lessons for dyslexia centre learning. But, even with all the knowledge she had acquired about this area of teaching, she was unaware of what learning programmes were used. She also explained that Steve had been identified as having 'borderline dyscalculia', but as there is no provision for this in the school, nothing much happened. She explained how they asked for Steve's maths teacher to attend the last Statement review, where it was agreed that he would have an extra ten minutes lesson. But Steve did not like this teacher, and after three weeks they stopped.

Steve felt that what he was learning at this school was 'what I need'. He thought that what he was learning was important for his GCSEs and for his future. He was satisfied with having foreign language lesson time to focus on his English. His parents noted that Steve was pleased when he had written something at length. His mother talked about how he had phoned home to say he had a good result: 'I don't think he could ever believe that he could ever get that sort of result.' Steve agreed with this himself: 'I feel like I can read anything I want to now, unlike two years ago . . . I was literally like hiding away from books . . . I've actually progressed so much in English since I started the dyslexia centre in year 6.' Steve also explained how writing was most challenging for him: 'I write down my work and then I'll come back to look at it a week later and I can't read it.' He now uses an iPad to type in his writing, and that has 'helped a lot with English'. He also said that he was 'mucking about in lessons' less as he sees his 'education as a bit more important'. His mother confirmed this connection between perception of his future and how he engages in school learning.

Teachers and teaching

Steve's teacher talked about the literacy programme they used as 'highly organized and structured', but they do not get too focused on literacy as they combine it with the mainstream English programme. He explained further that they do not use any particular programme to improve memory, but 'the way that we teach is trying to improve it'. However, he did believe that the 'strategies that you use with students like Steve, everyone benefits from'. But, he went on to explain that: 'with students like Steve you have to take it a little bit further. But the general things you're trying to do are good teaching strategies anyway.' He applied this to trainee or new teachers who were worried about teaching pupils with dyslexia; 'I tell them that there is no need to be, because if you are a good teacher, you will be a good teacher of dyslexic students.' Steve, in his own terms, expressed a similar view to this about the teaching he needed. He felt that teaching that involved activity and used visual methods were motivating for him, but relevant to others too.

Steve's teacher believed that the key factor in teaching pupils like Steve was not what they are taught, but how this is done and the relationship with them. For Steve he explained that he 'tried to get him on my side right from the word go, but it wasn't that easy to begin with. But I think now we're pretty much completely comfortable in each other's company and I think he trusts me.' Steve's parents thought that his teacher had 'that special relationship with his children . . . and it was impressive to watch'. They spoke of an episode where he had been responsive to Steve's needs concerning seeing the whiteboard. After an eye-check for Steve's headaches when he reads, no problems were found. But, it was suggested that the whiteboard might be changed to suit Steve, as he did not want to use tinted lenses. His teacher spoke to him about altering the whiteboard, but in the end Steve did not want this to happen because he did not want to be seen to alter the whiteboard for everyone else.

By contrast, Steve himself felt that his relationship with a teacher did not 'really matter' for his learning, though he had clear preferences about the teachers he liked and disliked.

Steve's parents had strong views about the training and skills of teachers: 'a lot of the things you can do for dyslexia can be good for basic readers anyway' and 'it's just simple things that can help so much'. For example, present something in a pictorial way, give homework printed on paper, not written on the board, have a cream board that will suit everyone. They felt that much of dyslexia help was not expensive and was about understanding and the training of teachers. Their experience at Steve's primary school reinforced these views – for example, their experience of a newly qualified teacher who did not have any sense of what to do. This contrasted with Steve's dyslexia centre teacher who moved from PE teaching to this line of teaching and had dyslexia-relevant qualifications from a well-respected university programme.

The challenge that Steve posed teachers, from his mother's perspective, was how to 'get him to sit down long enough . . . he's very much the quickest, the minimum amount possible . . . let's quickly scribble down something just to shut the teacher up'. She continues to support his learning by, for example, getting videos about the sciences and supporting the science revision. For Steve's teacher the key factor in enabling him to learn is being alert, as he can become easily tired. Steve also needs to learn and concentrate in short bursts involving interactive learning, according to his teacher. Steve's parents also recognized that he works best when activities and tasks are broken down into chunks. They also observed that using the iPad had helped him improve in subjects like geography and history. Steve's own views about what helps his learning agreed with what his parents and teacher thought: for example, interactive teaching where the teacher talks to the pupils rather than getting them to copy from the board, representing ideas visually not just talk about them, the use of the iPad, and a teacher who discussed learning with the pupils and found new interesting ways to present.

What school?

Steve's parents felt that Steve's current school was in many ways ideal because their twins were now 'not ashamed of being dyslexic and that's the joy of putting them in that environment'. For Steve, his current school was almost ideal: 'the best school . . . would be like this school and a little better'. Better for him would be slightly fewer in the dyslexia centre classes and a bigger sports area. The dyslexia centre was a main factor in him liking this school, but he also liked the boarding aspect, 'it's just so nice to be with them every day'.

Steve's teacher was reluctant to compare this fee-paying school with a state-funded secondary school with a dyslexia resource. For him, the key factor was whether there was the specialist provision. One advantage of this school compared to a large state-funded secondary school was that 'everyone knows everyone else . . . you can create a family atmosphere very easily'. Steve's parents had also considered a fee-paying specialist dyslexia school for their twins. Besides the higher fees, which the authority would have to pay, they wondered about the effect on pupils of being 'literally shut up with other dyslexics, most of them severe . . . they're in a world where everyone is dyslexic and it's not going to be like that when they get out . . . they're going to have such a shock'. They felt that this differed from the twins' current school where there are non-dyslexic pupils, which 'makes for a more normal sort of school for them'.

On the subject of specialized schools, Steve's teacher felt he had to be careful about what he said. He thought that a special school for dyslexic pupils would be very useful for 'a short-term burst – say a year or two of really concentrated, focused effort, mainly on the English language'. But, on the other hand, he felt that 'if a child can cope in an ordinary school then that's where they should go, simply because ultimately they have to be able to cope in the real world'. He also believed that there was 'a crying need' for schools like the one Steve was at, and this would grow with more pressure on pupils at GCSE. Steve's mother recognized some regrets that the twins were not at a state school because of the social side; them not having local friends. Steve does know people locally, but not ones they meet up with, aside from the rugby involvement. But she also recognized that he is now in a small school where he is protected from 'negative influences'. Steve had not heard about inclusion, but knew that integration meant mixing with others. When asked what he would feel if he went to a special school for pupils with dyslexia, he said that if others found out it would be awkward because it would label you, compared to coming to his current school, which did not.

Parental involvement

Steve's parents and his teacher felt that they had a good working relationship. Steve's teacher made an effort to keep in contact and commented that his parents' confidence in the school had grown. Steve's father believed that his wife's keeping up to date about dyslexia had made it possible to prevent the teachers from 'fobbing them off'. He also commented on the difference between the public and private sector as regards parental relationships. In the state primary school parents' evening were like 'speed dating', having 'five minutes with the allocated teacher'. At the twins' current school they offer you a drink and you are left thinking 'hold on . . . I've been with this teacher for 20 minutes. How do I get away?'

Steve's parents also believed that the private educational psychologist had helped, compared to the local authority ones, who act as if 'their hands are tied'. Steve's father said that when you confront the authority they say it is a monetary matter, but this went against the legislation. He felt that with the pressure they exerted, based mainly on his wife's research and partly his persistence, the authority was willing to change. Steve's mother wondered whether the authority 'wanted to wear you down so that you wouldn't go the whole way', saying that it was a 'constant fight', and they 'breathed a sigh of relief' when the current provision was initially agreed.

Steve's mother was a member of a local dyslexia association and attended all their courses. She also had had some support from a psychologist who was on the committee, such as advice about the reports for the Statement and about provision options. She found that these courses were attended much more by teachers than parents, and wondered if there could be some specifically for parents.

Social interaction

Steve's teacher described him as 'friendly . . . he's personable, sociable and he used to get a little bit too physical' in the past. He thought that this came from Steve becoming frustrated and over-responding – it was not bullying. But he felt that Steve had grown out of it. Steve also recognized that the adults at school knew him as 'causing a bit of trouble', but this hardly happened now. He explained this in terms of realizing that education was more important. His parents described him as 'one of the more popular members of the year group . . . that is his skill'. His father added that Steve was a leader and would 'be there at the front, and people will follow him'.

Steve described one of his best friends, who also had dyslexia, but he did not think having dyslexia was important to being friendly with someone. They both liked 'mucking about', and they both know what each other is like. He explained how they only see each other outside school occasionally as they live far apart. As regards relationships at home, he felt he got on better with some, like his older sister, than he did with others. He felt he got on with his parents 'all right', saying that he did not 'agree with them on everything'. Steve's mother confirmed Steve getting on well with his older sister, and said that he gets on quite well with his twin brother – but 'if there's an opportunity to not include Bob, he won't at all'. Yet, both parents commented that Steve, though the more outgoing of the two, leans heavily on his twin brother.

Future

Steve's teacher's main concern about his future was that, until he is a bit older, 'he needs to be in a supportive, caring environment that keeps quite a close eye on him'. So long as Steve was succeeding, he felt he would be all right; were he to start to struggle, 'I would fear for him.' Also, he would be concerned 'if he got into the wrong company'. Steve's father's concerns were less about his dyslexia than general teenage motivation issues, and that he will 'land wherever he does with the talents he's got'.

Steve's teacher could see him getting a decent set of GCSEs at C grades and going on to a vocational course: 'I've got a lot of confidence that he's going to do well.' Steve said that he was thinking more now about his GCSEs, feeling sometimes that: 'I really want to do well at GCSEs because I want a nice job.' His parents hoped that things will 'click with him' for his GCSEs. As regards a future occupation, Steve hardly talks about this to his parents. However, his mother said that the other day Steve had mentioned that he had thought about teaching sport. His own view was that he wanted to do something outdoors, perhaps something like a PE teacher. His father summarized his views in these terms: 'he's got abilities with his leadership. He needs, unfortunately, what I didn't have, which is to get bits of paper behind him. So I hope he does crack on and do that.'

6
Jon

Mother: *For parents*: 'Speak up and speak out, if they could truly believe something in their heart of hearts they'd speak up for their children. 'Cause I kept quiet for a few years wanting help and it didn't get me anywhere.'

For teachers: 'Listen to what parents say and take parents' views and thoughts seriously, rather than them doing what they think is right, because that won't work.'

Background information

Jon who is 6 years old lives with his mother and older sister, who is 11, in an urban area. Jon has never had any contact with his father. He goes daily to an off-site unit for children and young people with social and emotional difficulties after having been excluded from his primary school. His mother was interviewed at home. Jon's care support assistant was interviewed briefly at the unit, but this was cut short because Jon did not want to be away from him. Jon and his care support assistant then talked while we, the three of us, went for a walk in the woods outside the unit.

Identification

Jon's mother first noticed that Jon reacted to smells when he was a toddler. He covered his nose when there were strong smells around. At that stage he began to have temper tantrums. For example, when he was playing with blocks and things did not go 'his way, he would just smash up the bricks or blocks'. When playing with a car, if it did not go in the direction he wanted, he reacted to this too.

Soon after Jon started at nursery, at 3 years old, there were concerns about his behaviour, so Common Assessment Framework meetings (a multi-professional monitoring of children with additional needs) were started. This resulted in them using a 'traffic-light' chart, to record how each day went. For example, if he was on red, then it had not been a good day. She recalls that they used a timer and at times he was put in a room by himself. This was the support that was provided. Jon's mother requested an educational psychologist assessment a few times from the school in his reception year, but no psychologist became involved. She only realized later that she could have requested this assessment directly without the school's involvement. It was about six months before the interview with her that Jon's mother finally received a psychologist's report. She discussed how the psychologist in this report had picked up Jon's sensory issues, his attachment difficulties and how he struggles in larger groups of children. Jon's mother was relieved to get the report because it recorded what 'school hadn't picked up in three and a half years'.

A paediatrician had been involved too and the Connors ADHD questionnaire had been used. When she completed the questionnaire she scored his behaviour at a high level of difficulties, but Jon's behaviour had been calm over the period that his teachers completed it. So, Jon's Connors score was low for school and a diagnosis of ADHD was not pursued. In addition, an assessment for autism was conducted for Jon, but nothing came of that.

At the time of the interview, his mother described him as liking to draw, read and write, but he 'lacked in confidence and concentration, he doesn't stick to one thing'. He was also described as liking to swim. For his mother, Jon's main difficulties were about sitting and doing an activity for a period of time. He tended to flit to something else. Nor did he like to be told what to do; 'it's his way or no way'. His mother also described him becoming 'really attached to people' and, if attached to someone, he wanted to be with them constantly. He continued to have an aversion to certain smells to the point where he becomes physically sick.

At school, when he has 'meltdowns . . . he tends to go under a blanket and hide away; he liked to be on his own'. Though he does like playing with other children, he struggles to do so without some problem. At home he can be 'very defiant, very angry'. He becomes violent, can 'smash up the house', and his mother described his swearing as 'absolutely appalling'. The smallest little thing can 'trigger him off – any sort of change', as his mother explained. Jon finds change difficult to cope with, so 'you've got to prepare him every step of the way and if you change any of it he just goes boom and he's gone'. His mother had also noticed that when Jon is 'close to somebody, that's who he hurts'. In public he can also hit out 'if people are in his way and he's in meltdown mode'.

Jon's care assistant described Jon as a 'very loving and caring boy, but at the same time he can be very aggressive . . . if he doesn't get his own way'. His assistant believed that these problems tended to occur more when Jon was tired. This depended on how he slept at home; Jon slept with his mother because of his problems in sleeping. He also noticed that towards the end of the week Jon became more tired and found it more difficult to engage in activities. His assistant also noted a similar pattern of behaviour in the unit to that which his mother described at home; if he does not get what he wants, he becomes aggressive. But his assistant also noted that sometimes, even if he gets his own way, there can be an aggressive outburst about 'nothing at all'.

Jon's assistant described him as 'intelligent' and very capable at reading for his age. But, he will apply himself only if it interests him. His assistant asked Jon to count to 60 during our walk, which he did very fluently and without error. Jon had only been at the unit for five months and, according to his assistant, Jon's behaviour had improved since then. When he first came to the unit, if he was asked to do something, he could have a 'temper outburst'. But, more recently, Jon was less inclined to behave like this.

Causes

Jon's mother described how Jon told her that sometimes he 'can't help being naughty'. He had also told her that sometimes he did not even know that he was being 'naughty'. But he was aware of the consequences of his behaviour; he had told her that 'they're just going to kick me out again like they did last time'. Jon's mother described how when 'he had a meltdown his eyes were glazed over and he's completely gone – shut down'. She felt that 'he can't control being naughty'.

She had strong concerns when Jon was at primary school that his behaviour was getting worse – for example, with incidents such as pulling books off the library shelves. It was then that she felt that 'we need to do something now to prevent this' and mentioned how she told the teacher that, 'if you don't do something now, like follow the ed psych report, what they've told you, we're going to be in serious trouble'. The teacher's response was that he was not at risk of exclusion and that they had 'worse children than him'. Then, a week later, he was permanently excluded. From her perspective, this was unjustified as exclusion should be a last resort and not enough had been done to prevent these incidents.

Both Jon's mother and his assistant talked about his anxieties. Getting dressed in the morning could be an issue. His mother described how Jon could not dress himself fully. She saw this as a problem of delayed coordination. She would help him dress in the mornings for school to avoid a 'meltdown'. She realized that this sounded 'awful', but justified it as 'trying to get him off on a good start to the day'. By himself he might put his sock on the wrong way or his pants the wrong way round. But she was not sure 'what the answer is because I don't know what I'm dealing with'. She also discussed how he became upset about failing; 'he does not like getting anything wrong'. Jon's assistant wondered whether Jon's anxiety arose from what went on at home.

Impact

Jon's mother believed that Jon's behaviour difficulties impacted on him very significantly. He was described as becoming very tearful and angry about the difficult situations. She described him as frightened about going back to school, when she raises the topic with him. She described him as feeling he had failed and frightened about what will happen. She also felt that he was angry with himself and about what happened at school when he was excluded. Jon had felt that his views about what happened had not been listened to. Jon's assistant also talked about Jon referring back to negative incidents if he was having a 'bad day'. He could also refer back to negative incidents when he does not want to do something.

Jon's mother also talked about how these behaviour difficulties had adversely affected her; the worry and concerns had made her feel 'poorly'. She felt that she and Jon have been 'failed' because nobody had listened to them or put provision in place. The difficulties had also affected Jon's older sister, who had learned to shut herself away in her room when there was an outburst. Jon's mother thought that her daughter was upset because she spent so much time with Jon and had little time to focus on her daughter. Jon's assistant also described some negative effects of these behaviour difficulties. Jon's mother had told him that her friends and neighbours did not understand Jon's behaviour. For example, a neighbour had threatened to call the police when Jon was in crisis. Jon's mother also described how she had no family support with Jon, something that was left to her to deal with, especially since her mother had died.

Labels

Jon's mother described the terms that have been used for Jon: 'defiant, extreme, complex . . . and severe behavioural difficulties'. She also felt that he was labelled by others to the extent that if 'anything goes wrong he will be blamed'. If there was an incident with Jon and another child 'even if it might not be his fault . . . it will always be his fault'. She has told Jon to tell the teacher if there was an incident when another child was 'being horrible' to him. From what she could find out from Jon, when he did this, the teacher would usually tell him to 'go away and stop telling tales'.

Jon's mother believed that there was 'an underlying something' that explained his behaviour – something 'along a spectrum like ADHD'. She also wondered if with his sensory responses being 'so extreme' and his strong attachments, 'it's on the autistic spectrum of some sort', but she was not sure about this. Jon's assistant mentioned that his mother believed initially that Jon had ADHD. He saw her as looking for an explanation of his behaviour difficulties. For him, this was an example of the need for firm boundaries and structure needing to be put in place.

Statement

At the time of the interviews Jon did not have a Statement, even though his mother had wanted one since the difficulties started. The reason she was given was that 'there's so much backlog and that he didn't show the behaviours as badly at school as he did at home'. She did not realize till the Information and Advisory worker told her that she could request a Statement herself. But, by the time she knew about this, 'it was too late'.

But Jon's mother had just heard that they were about to start the statutory assessment for him to be issued an EHC Plan. She hoped that the Plan would provide the 'right support that he has clearly needed since day dot, but sadly nothing was done'. She knew that she would provide a report herself for the assessment process, but had also been asked in the letter to her to ask other professionals to provide their reports. She felt that she had enough to do without having to ask some professionals for their reports to be sent to the education office. The only advice and support she had had over the assessment process came from the Information and Advisory worker.

Mental health support

Jon's mother went into more detail about her not having had any support for him till he went into the nursery, despite her going many times to see doctors and health visitors. She described how a health visitor came to the home a couple of years ago and observed almost two hours of Jon 'attacking' her. Based on this the health visitor referred them on to a social worker to consider whether Jon could be identified as a 'child in need'. However, it was decided, as Jon's mother explained, that Jon was not a child 'in need' as she was a 'good mother and there were no concerns for the child's welfare'.

Learning: what and how

Previous provision

When Jon was in the reception year at primary school he did take part in some Thrive activities (which aim to enhance relationships between child and adults). The programme was, however, run in a little hut at a nearby secondary school every day for half a day. Jon was described as 'coming on in leaps and bounds', till about half way through the reception year there was an incident which meant that Jon was considered to be a risk to himself and others. This resulted in him only receiving Thrive activities for an hour a day.

During Jon's last year at primary school he was supported by a male teaching assistant to whom he became very attached. This assistant was, according to Jon's mother, very friendly to him: it was as if 'they were best buddies . . . you could see the relationship between them'. Jon was described as 'besotted with him . . . he just absolutely loved him'. If his mother asked Jon why he liked this assistant, Jon said 'because he's nice to me; because he listens to me'. This relationship was noted in the educational psychologist's report. For Jon's mother this showed what Jon needed – somebody with 'a lot of patience and a lot of time for him'. But, she realized that this assistant was not employed for Jon as he was the general class assistant. When Jon's mother talks to Jon now about going back to school he says he wants to go back to be with this assistant, not to the teacher he had. This was a cause of concern for his mother about him returning to this school.

The incident five months before the interview that led to Jon's exclusion involved him slamming the lid of a piano on the teacher's hand. For his mother, this was a one-off event, and there had been no previous incidents when 'he was violent with any pupils or staff'. Before the incident he had broken things in the classroom and thrown objects around. It was an increase of this behaviour that led her to express her concerns at school the week before the excluding incident.

Current provision

Jon spent the mornings at the off-site provision with a care assistant (he had a main assistant for three days and two others, each a day a week) and in the afternoons he had two hours' tutorial with teachers. His mother had some doubts about whether this was the right provision for him. She wondered if the deterioration in his behaviour was due to what he observed in the unit where he mixed with older children: 'sadly his behaviour has deteriorated a hell of a lot more because of the environment he's in, he's witnessing things'. For her this made it even more unlikely he would return to ordinary school. However, she did believe that it was the right provision, as he 'gets the one-to-one help and plenty of Thrive, which is what he needs'. She was also worried that Jon did not understand why he was not at school and that he only had two hours' tutorial a day.

She appreciated the relationship that had built up between Jon and his key support assistant, but had some concerns about whether Jon would feel let down when he left the unit. She felt that Jon needed to gradually reduce his contact with the assistant when he leaves to avoid a negative reaction to the separation. How Jon related to his assistant was evident when we walked in the woods. Jon was responsive to his assistant – for example, when Jon asked to go into an enclosure, the assistant said no, and Jon accepted this.

Jon' s mother recognized that Jon was more responsive to men, but she wondered about some negative effects of having three different assistants in a week. She also realized how his behaviour fluctuated between 'being an absolute diamond' to being 'awful with them, with swearing and hitting'. She also understood Jon's behaviour in terms of trust: if 'he trusts them, he was fine', but 'if their attention went to somebody else when he wanted their attention' there would be trouble. She discussed a recent incident with Jon's key assistant when they were out in town. The assistant had parked the car outside a park where there were swings. Jon wanted to go on the swings, but his assistant said he could go only after they had had a walk. This was the trigger for Jon to hit out and kick his assistant, who could not restrain him, so he called the unit for someone else to come to his assistance.

Jon's assistant saw the situation with Jon as one where the unit needed to work with his mother to put in place some structure and consistency at home. For him, Jon required a consistent approach with boundaries and clear consequences for his behaviour.

School learning: what helps and hinders

Jon's mother said that Jon said that he missed his school friends and that he did not want to do 'school work at the unit . . . cause it's not a proper school'. Jon was reported as saying: 'Why should I do school work, it's not a proper school?' His mother realized that his learning progress had been affected by his behavioural difficulties in class. The key issue was 'getting him to do it . . . it's having the right people – like the ed psych report does say – he did need small groups'. She went on to explain that 'if he doesn't get his way it is full on meltdown mode that could last anything from ten minutes up to hours'. She felt that it was important that he learned to carry out instructions, but as the professional reports said, he was 'emotionally like a 2-year-old'.

When Jon's mother was asked what was ideal provision for him, she referred to the psychologist's report which she read out aloud to me. This was about emotional literacy and regulation, adult containing and not escalating negative reactions, and modelling how to handle emotions without confrontations. For his mother this was very helpful advice from a psychologist who had visited Jon several times.

In terms of what helps his learning, his mother believed that he needed consistent praise and managing, and regular prompting for most activities because 'he's so easily distracted that he'll go from one thing straight to another'. He also needed adult patience and understanding; that it is all right to feel sad. She thought that he became angry when he made a mistake and starts to think that 'because . . . he's done it wrong, he can't do it any more'. She also believed that he did much better in small groups, as the educational psychologist had confirmed in her report about Jon. His mother also believed that he responded better to a limited choice between two options than open choices.

Placement

Current placement

The off-site unit which Jon attended was about 40 minutes' drive from his house. He was picked up and dropped off each day by his key care support assistant. The placement at the unit was meant to be for a temporary period with the aim of Jon returning to an ordinary school. His support assistant believed that Jon could eventually return to the mainstream, not initially into a classroom environment but in a small group or one-to-one setting.

Jon's mother had considered that Jon might go to another ordinary school because Jon had 'lost trust in the teachers' at his previous school. She talked about seven teachers who became involved in the incident. She also felt that 'they had told lies' about Jon. On the other hand, Jon had some friends at this school and he might struggle to make new friends at a new school.

Jon's support assistant talked during his interview about a recent meeting about Jon's reintegration back to his previous school which did not include his mother. The school's SEN coordinator was going to visit the unit to work with Jon as part of a phased return to the school. His mother expressed her concerns about him going back without the right plan and support being in place. There was an upcoming meeting about Jon which she was going to attend and where she planned to express her concerns about a mainstream school coping with Jon when she knew that the unit, a specialist provision, was 'struggling'.

Jon's mother mentioned that the Information and Advisory Service person and someone from the mental health service had said several times that Jon might 'not cope in a mainstream school'. She was not interested in a residential special school where Jon slept away from home, because of his sleeping problems. However, she also had concerns that 'if he goes to a specialist provision he's never going to get any better . . . he'll just pick up on other negative behaviours'.

When Jon's mother thought about the school placement decisions she recalled that she used to believe that as 'a normal child, he could go to school'. But, she said that she had begun to 'take a step back now and look at the bigger picture'; she would see other people's viewpoints when they see his 'swearing, with his threats to kill' in the mainstream school. So, she said that she would now accept this option, compared to several months ago when she believed 'absolutely not . . . he's going back to mainstream school'. Her worry was that she might be setting Jon up to fail were he to go to a mainstream school: 'if the unit are struggling with his behaviour there where they're trained, how are they going to cope in a mainstream school?' She expanded on this in these terms: 'I can't afford for an incident to kick off in the school, them not be able to support Jon, and then we're back to square one being suspended again'. She summarized the hard decision she has to make in these terms: in a specialist setting 'he'll get the right support . . . I think he'll get the right support. But I also feel, in another sense . . . how do we know it's not going to work with the right support in place in a mainstream school?'

Parental involvement

After the exclusion incident Jon's mother had approached a solicitor, someone she knew from her own school, about what happened, to see if there was anything she could do about the way the school treated Jon. She felt that Jon 'had been failed left, right and centre all the way through . . . I thought the school was doing enough and I put a lot of trust and faith in the school that I could put my son's life in their hands, and they failed us both'. One of the reasons she depended on the school was that she had received no support from mental health and local authority support services over the last few years. She described how Jon was described as 'very complex and very defiant', that they said they had 'huge concerns', but they said that there was nothing they could do. She felt that they had 'been discharged to nowhere and left . . . which was why I've fallen back on the school because at the time I thought they were completely supportive of everything, but now I've realized there wasn't enough done'. She also came to realize that she did not know enough about the local planning system for children like Jon, and nobody had informed her about it, though she did eventually find out about it from the Information and Advisory Service person.

The outcome of going to a solicitor was that a letter was written to the school complaining that the exclusion decision was not taken as a last resort, and they had not done enough before this decision for Jon. They had not asked Jon what his views were about the exclusion incident. Another issue raised with the school was why had the educational psychologist's report not been followed through. Jon's mother believed that the teachers had not prepared themselves about 'how to handle Jon and it was all handled wrong, and sadly he's a hell of a lot worse now'. She was under the impression until quite recently that they realized they had failed. But, she believed that they then tried 'to turn it around on to me, so it looks bad on me'. The social worker involved, according to Jon's mother, was told that Jon's mother had declined help and had not been cooperative, even though she had been to the two assessment meetings. She had also been accused of saying at the meeting that she would put comments about the school on Facebook, which she denied having said. Her solicitor was at the meeting and she confirmed that Jon's mother had not said she would put a message on Facebook about the school. In addition, minutes were not taken at the two assessment meetings which was witnessed by her Information and Advisory Service worker. The school then produced the minutes for the two meetings. This was the background to Jon's mother's concerns about what went on 'behind closed doors', so that her 'trust, confidence, faith, communication, the whole lot has just completely gone. And do I want my son in that environment?'

She was adamant that she was not going to drop the complaint as the events had a 'massive impact on her family'. She had not felt well, cried a lot, and had to struggle with Jon's behaviour. All this had been aggravated till she felt bad enough to take anti-depressants: 'I didn't want it coming to that, but I'm struggling to keep on board with it, all because they're knocking me down with lies being told, then I pick myself up and then another lie comes on and I'm bobbing up and down.' She also expressed that she was 'mortified' because she believed that 'by law they should have asked Jon what happened, but they didn't ask him at all'. A meeting had now been arranged with the school governors in two weeks' time. She was hoping that the school apologizes: 'put their hands up and accept that they've done wrong'.

Jon's mother also discussed how staff from the unit worked closely with her over Jon's needs. She felt that she had a 'good relationship' with them which involved discussing what might or might not work with Jon'. It was clear that she valued this working relationship in supporting her at home with respect to managing Jon's behaviour. She also felt that the reason why the teachers at his previous school did not relate like this to her was because it was 'too time-consuming'.

Jon's mother found herself in a situation where she was being supported both by an Information and Advisory Service worker and a solicitor. However, the Information and Advisory worker would not be involved in meetings where the solicitor was present. So, she organized for the Advice worker to come to the assessment meetings, while the solicitor dealt with the complaint matter. She was very positive about the support she received from them both. She described the Information and Advisory Service worker as 'absolutely fantastic . . . cannot praise her enough; she is the lady I phone Monday, Tuesday, Thursday. She is at the end of the phone, she's heard me sobbing, she's . . . But she's lifted my spirits saying "We will get there."' She also gave her information about clubs and other activities for Jon to do outside school time. Jon's mother described how she struggles during the school holidays when Jon is at home all day. She described her solicitor as 'her rock'. However, Jon's mother did not belong to any parent support group, getting support from these two people.

Social interaction

Jon's mother described how Jon could engage with other children in the park or a play area, but mainly with younger children. With them he could take turns and let them have a ride and sometimes be 'compassionate'. His mother believed that he could make friendships but found it hard to keep friends. Jon is quite tall and strong for his age, so he can sometimes intimidate other children. His mother felt that he played with younger children because he was emotionally immature. She also believed that it was also about power: 'if he says to a younger person "I want that", then he will get that'.

Jon's relationship with his older sister was described by his mother as close. But, she also felt that he hurts those who are close to him, so he might hit, punch, kick or bite her. His sister would stand there and let him do it. His mother became cross with her daughter for letting this happen, telling her that she should stand up for herself.

Future

Jon's mother felt that 'if we don't get the right support we're going to spiral out and it's going to be a lot worse'. She had doubts about Jon improving without professional help, whether 'it's a diagnosis or whether it's the right support in place'.

She worried that if this did not happen and 'we plod on like we are now, I wouldn't even like to say where we're going to be in three years' time'. She mentioned talking to some police about future problems 'if people don't start helping'. Her concerns were about Jon becoming stronger and 'getting more weight behind him when he slaps or punches'. Her hopes were confined to finding 'the right support'. She felt this kind of support was along the lines of what he received in the off-site unit, but with more teaching input. She did realize, despite these hopes, that Jon 'doesn't cope very well within school settings, so I don't know what the answer is'.

7
Sandy

Mother: 'You have to send your child to school so therefore they have to provide it . . . if they think they need something then they need to provide for that need. If I had my time again I'd pull her out . . . I would have de-registered her . . . I just think it's about questioning, isn't it?'

Teaching assistant: 'It's actually getting to know that child really, really well . . . what makes them tick. Write it down 'cause then you can look back and say "Well actually this happened – that was the result; that's what triggered it."'

'This child is struggling in school. This child has got issues with school. Let's get somebody in. Let's try and make it easier for them. I think by the time you get to 5, 6 or 7, those children have lost all that time, and actually are they in the right place?'

Background information

Sandy, 12 years old, lived in an urban area with her mother, step-father and younger 7-year-old brother. She had recently moved to a residential special school for children with complex emotional and behavioural needs, which she went to after spending short periods at two special schools following a longer period at the local primary school. She came home every half term. Sandy and her mother were interviewed at home, and her primary teaching assistant at the school.

Identification of needs

Strengths and difficulties

Sandy's mother described Sandy's behaviour as 'always very busy, even at nursery', but she also felt that Sandy was 'very bright and intelligent'. Sandy was described as thinking that 'she's more grown up than she is', resulting in a clash between her mental and emotional development. She contrasted Sandy with her son, who was described as getting on 'fine'.

Sandy's mother understood the problems in terms of Sandy being controlling; 'she likes to do what she likes to do; I don't think she means to be bullish, she doesn't know any other way'. As Sandy became older 'it's got harder and harder because nothing has happened and all the way through we've just been treading water. All these people get involved and nothing changes.'

Sandy was described as having difficulties during her nursery years in sitting down and being with other children. She would roll around, which others saw as 'cute'. But, when it continued into the primary years these behaviours came to be seen as more of an issue. Her mother thought at the time that Sandy had a language comprehension difficulty based on her observation that despite speaking so well, she had problems finding the right word. Yet, Sandy was reading and writing before she started school.

Sandy's mother described Sandy as having an outgoing personality and loving school. But she missed out on activities like school trips because of her 'naughty' behaviour. Her mother also suspected that Sandy was not as confident as she presented; 'she's very insecure . . . she needs her self-esteem building'. This was evident in her wanting to be the centre of attention. So, as her mother explained, 'whatever was happening in the classroom, she'd bring it back to herself'.

Her assistant confirmed this picture of Sandy as insecure about herself. Despite reassurance, Sandy would frequently say, 'I hate myself. I'm fat, I'm ugly.' Sandy had fine hair when she was younger which did not grow as long as the other girls' hair. So, one day, as the assistant explained, Sandy decided to cut her hair, saying: 'Oh I hate my hair . . . it's never going to grow.' Her assistant also described another incident that she felt reflected Sandy's issues about empathy with other children and her need to be the centre of attention. The assistant explained that when children fall down in the playground, other children often run over and help them up. Sandy was described as not doing this, but rather falling over herself to see if others would come to her help.

Sandy had both eczema and asthma. She had also had problems with her ears, having had three lots of grommets and adenoids. Her mother wondered whether some of the teachers knew that Sandy might at times not be able to hear. Her mother thought that Sandy's tendency to be loud and shout might be because of her hearing difficulties. On the other hand, her mother commented that Sandy could say things that others did not like. Tact was an issue for her, and when her mother suggested she 'put herself in someone else's shoes', Sandy replied that if she did this, 'I'll get verrucas'.

She needed, her mother believed, to 'stop for a minute . . . as she does not think of consequences until it's too late'. The teaching assistant talked about incidents when Sandy ran out of school, dancing in the road on a very busy road, to illustrate how hard it was to keep her safe. Sandy's mother explained that Sandy could be apologetic, but 'she thinks you're having a go at her when you try to talk about it . . . her feelings are what matter . . . she can't step out of that and think that there are other people's feelings involved as well'. Her teaching assistant described an incident at school when Sandy showed little regret when she upset others. In this incident the other children were removed from the classroom because Sandy started to kick a toughened glass door. She ignored this and kicked it through. As the assistant explained, 'it worried us that she would not see the dangers in things . . . that she couldn't or she wouldn't'.

However, her teaching assistant also recognized that on a one-to-one basis Sandy 'had a side of herself that she doesn't show to very many people'. Sandy had 'a really good sense of fun, good sense of humour . . . she can be quite affectionate and happy'. But, in the classroom environment, Sandy was described as a 'completely different child'. From her teaching assistant's perspective, Sandy was more composed when she was in a one-to-one situation away from everybody else, where she did not have to compete and she did things at her own pace. Sandy was also described as very capable at games like tag rugby, and she really got involved in activities like gymnastics.

There was also a period when Sandy would take pins and stick them in her arms and legs. This was related to her eczema, and she would pick at her skin till it bled. Sometimes she had also used headbanging and, on one occasion when 6 years old, she stabbed another teaching assistant with a pencil. She sharpened the pencil first and stabbed the assistant twice with it. This was an assistant she usually liked very much. Sandy's mother also talked about Sandy's picking at her scabs, though she commented that this had stopped more recently. There were also incidents where Sandy would say that she could not breathe and her mother did not know if this was a genuine issue or not. The school told her mother to take Sandy home when this happened and take her to hospital. When her mother took Sandy to the hospital the staff there began to ask questions about what was going on as she was repeatedly going there.

Sandy's mother believed that if Sandy's problems had been handled a while ago, Sandy would have made much more progress in her learning. Sandy's teaching assistant also believed that had Sandy not been frequently out of the class and excluded from school and 'put her mind to it', she could have been expected to achieve level 5s in the year 6 SATs. The assistant's point was that Sandy had the abilities to achieve, especially in maths, which was her favourite subject at primary school. Sandy's literacy was at a slightly lower level, but the main factor that undermined her progress was an 'I need to get it done quickly' attitude, and she did not accept correction easily.

Sandy was also known to screw up the paper that she wrote on, so the teachers did not give her exercise books to write in. Once Sandy had completed some work, her assistant used to photocopy the paper to keep a copy. Another example was mental maths; if the maths questions were read out too quickly, this could become a 'blow point for her'. So it was decided that mental maths would be done somewhere quiet, giving her adequate time to answer the questions. Though Sandy would get the questions right with more time, she felt it was unfair to be away from her peers.

Her assistant believed that nobody could 'pinpoint' what triggered Sandy's mood changes; she could come into school and 'be really disruptive from the minute she walked in the door, where she would literally run circles round us all day'. They decided after a while to not use the 'no' word with her and found that this strategy tended to work quite well.

There had been one period for about six months when Sandy, aged 8, was not involved in any challenging behaviours. Her family were going on vacation and her mother said to Sandy that she would not be able to come with them unless her behaviour improved. The mother booked the holiday and told Sandy that she 'had to sort herself out' for six months. Despite a few minor incidents, the effect on her behaviour was noticeable. Her assistant commented that 'everybody had assumed that she'd gone on to Ritalin or something like that'. This prompted people to ask about the behaviour change, but her assistant realized that for Sandy this was a considerable effort which she could not keep up. They all went on holiday, but when they returned Sandy was described 'as worse than ever'.

During her interview Sandy was able to talk about herself: 'if someone messes me about . . . I'll probably just like kick off'. She said that this tended not to happen at home as nobody 'annoyed her there'. The 'kicking off' had taken place at her primary school and only sometimes at her new residential school. As for her school learning, Sandy felt that she was 'good at English, maths and food tech'. She felt that she got on well with her brother and had quite a few friends (two of whom were sitting in her bedroom during the interview). But, when asked what they might think about her, she was ambivalent, wondering whether it was 'a lot of horrible stuff' or that she was 'always there for them'.

Causes

During her interview Sandy could discuss what she felt made her annoyed and angry. This was when others swear at her and when 'people say they're going to do stuff and they don't'. She recognized that she had a difficulty with anger and that she got 'worked up and then it just explodes' and this feels like 'a bomb is going to go off inside me'. After such incidents she eventually stopped, and sometimes this may be because someone helps her calm down. What has helped her relax is to sit by herself for a while or go for a walk.

For Sandy's mother, discipline was a crucial issue. She felt that she could not give Sandy the routine she needs because of the situation they were in. She and her partner were working so it was difficult to have home routines. Others say that she could do this and that, but the issues keep going on and she felt 'worn out'. She felt that Sandy's behaviour was mostly not deliberate. The causes were to do with Sandy lacking some understanding and emotions. She likened the situation to 'telling someone with Tourette's not to swear . . . they can't help it'.

Sandy's teaching assistant, when reflecting about the causes, talked about some people thinking that Sandy did not hear well in class, at the time when she had the grommets done. But, from her own perspective, she considered that Sandy sometimes took offence when competing with her peers, e.g. racing to the door. But she also considered that Sandy struggled to experience empathy for others. The example she gave was when a child in her class had broken a wrist and then, within 24 hours, Sandy had hurt herself too, e.g. fallen down on the floor, and insisted that she needed a plaster cast, so needing to go to casualty. Though Sandy had not broken anything, she would then come into school with bandages on her arms and legs. When asked what had happened, she replied 'Oh, it's for my eczema.' Though she did have eczema, this was a bid for attention, in the assistant's view.

Impact

Sandy explained that her anger and breaking things 'doesn't really affect me'. However, there were consequences – for example, not using her phone or 'sanctions, like cleaning the windows'. Sandy's mother thought that Sandy knows that her challenging behaviour was 'not right'. Also, 'she knows she needs help, but she doesn't know what that help is'. Sandy accepted going to residential school because it was either that or home education, and she did not want to be at home.

Sandy's mother also explained how sometimes she signed off work because she felt unable to cope with what was going on. Her mother described how, at some point, she was being 'dragged out of work daily'. There had been police involvement following Sandy's brief placement at two schools that could not manage her. She felt that she was dealing with things that 'I shouldn't be dealing with, and these people that are helping me are not helping, they're making my life hard and worse.' She felt this adversely affected her parenting her younger son.

Sandy's mother explained how Sandy's brother gives in when Sandy wants something. For Sandy it is about control and her brother feels it is easier 'to let her have it'. Sandy's assistant described Sandy's parents as being 'at their wits end about what to do with her', but 'very supportive of the school'. Sandy herself recognized that her behaviour affected her mother, though she was awkward when talking about this and denied her brother understood what was going on as he was too young to understand.

Labels

Sandy's mother talked about how professionals had used the ADHD (attention deficit hyperactivity disorder) label for Sandy, about which she felt uneasy. In her view, 'they've put so many labels on her that they're creating a monster . . . they're making her feel like there's something wrong with her'. Subsequently they used the ODD label (opposition and defiance disorder) and, more recently, 'attachment disorder'. She did not find the labels useful, believing that 'we're labelling kids . . . I think they're products of society and we're too quick to put it on them'. She remembers when she was a child that she did some of the things Sandy has done, e.g. handstands on the couch, saying it was seen as normal then. However, she recognized that though Sandy had been 'constantly busy', she could also 'sit and do things if she wants to, so she's quite capable'. In her view, Sandy needed 'to be made to do it, and that's the problem . . . she needed the discipline; to me she needed a little bit of, "You're not going anywhere until you've finished it."' Her mother's attitude to labels was that the professionals were too quick in using them: they 'come in, they make an assessment . . . and walk away . . . and they don't realize what they've just left behind, and the knock-on effect' of using the label.

Sandy's teaching assistant remembered several different category labels being used for Sandy's behaviour, including ADHD and ODD. However, she felt that after working for more than 20 years with children with SEN, including autism and challenging behaviour, she believed that 'you couldn't really put Sandy in any particular category; it would be like trying to put a square peg in a round hole . . . she is unique'. When Sandy was interviewed, she knew the term 'special needs', giving examples of areas of difficulty, like ADHD, autism and so on. But she was unable to talk about whether she had special needs.

Statement

Sandy was issued with a Statement when she was 9 years old. However, her mother explained how, when she went to meetings about Sandy with professionals, she did not understand what was happening nor understand the significance of a Statement. It was explained that the Statement was 'all about funding' rather than being about Sandy and her personal needs. For her mother, it had been a 'fight'. Nor had Sandy's mother been told about the change to Education, Health and Care (EHC) Plans: 'to me it's just terms isn't it?' For her 'nothing gets done, that's my honest opinion . . . And I think it need not cost everything it does cost, you could streamline it and there's things they could do that they don't'. She was sceptical about holding the local authority to account through going to Tribunal. For her, 'I've been fighting all the way through and we still didn't get anything . . . You get picked up when it suits them and dropped when it suits them, but you've got to be there for their beck and call. And that's how I feel . . . I feel they've just totally invaded our life.'

Mental Health Service interventions

Sandy's mother talked about how the psychiatrist had put Sandy on a drug for ADHD. But, she was not happy about this, wanting them to try something like Cognitive Behavioural Therapy (CBT), mainly because she felt that Sandy needed understanding and talking. She said that she felt bad that she could not talk with Sandy about her emotions. The drug was justified by the psychiatrist who said that they could not help Sandy 'until she was helpable'. Sandy was also not keen to take the drug, and only did so for three months. Sandy's mother could not understand why the primary school did not have an observation room so parents could see what the teachers were dealing with. She also wanted other approaches to be tried which would cost less, such as a 'boot camp for a week'. She thought that Sandy needed 'to be broken', but would come to feel good when she completed the programme. Instead, they offered her parenting classes. Sandy's assistant did not recall any lead professional who gave direction to what was provided for Sandy. When Sandy was interviewed she said that nobody had met with her over the years and talked to her about what she got angry about. She said that she was not against talking with someone and would agree to sit down and talk with someone, were this available.

Learning: what and how

Current education provision

Sandy's mother was pleased with her provision at the residential special school, feeling that there had been a noticeable improvement in Sandy's behaviour, with her becoming calmer and pulling back in situations when she might have had an outburst. She had also received detailed reports and analysis of Sandy's school behaviour.

She preferred the system used in this special school to the previous special school which Sandy attended briefly. She liked the way they kept the children busy all day and they do not reward them 'every five minutes' whether they did something or not. She also liked the way the staff sit with the children after an incident and go through it with them, asking about their feelings and talking to them.

From Sandy's perspective food tech was her favourite school subject, mainly because she liked cooking. She talked about a range of subjects like history, religious education, physical education, maths and English. She also mentioned that they were due to do some social skills lessons sometime in the future. The best part of her school experience was her friends and some teachers. She talked about one of her teaching assistants as someone she really liked.

Primary school

Sandy's mother felt that Sandy's primary school had tried their best with her, but Sandy was rarely in the classroom with other children. At first her mother had not realized that this was the teaching arrangement. Sandy had been excluded many times over the last few years before she left the school for special school (four times in 2010, twice in 2011 and five in 2012). Sandy's mother recognized that the school did not want to exclude Sandy as they liked her, appreciating that she was likeable, had a good sense of humour and was funny. But Sandy's mother could not understand why the teacher would not put Sandy in a cupboard room for ten minutes when she was 'naughty'. She did not see this as a form of abuse.

Sandy's assistant explained how the small teaching room arose. They tried it for a month and it seemed to work. Sandy was 'calmer in the school and she seemed to like it'. Sandy would return to her class when they knew that she would not fail – for example, in PE, but not competitive sports. Gradually they built up the time in class so she could spend afternoons back in the class. This room, called the 'sanctuary', had some of Sandy's things and was where Sandy met her assistant at the start of the school day. This gave them 'a chance to talk about the morning and what happened last night and get her to a calm place'. Sometimes one or two other children, usually her friends, would join her in the sanctuary for a group-learning experience.

Important to learn

Sandy's assistant used to teach SEAL (social and emotional aspects of learning) activities with Sandy in a group context, in a way that addressed some of Sandy's issues with anger management. She also did activities like those associated with the Thrive programme (one that aims to enhance relationships between child and adults) for Sandy to express her feelings more constructively and to relieve stress and anxiety. Sandy's mother wanted a programme which would help Sandy to think about things; she spoke very positively about De Bono's approach to problem-solving as the kind of approach that she had in mind. Overall she felt that Sandy had the same basic needs as other children as Sandy was, in her view, capable of doing what was expected of her academically, but they also 'needed to tackle the emotional side'. What was needed was to have somebody with her to observe her when she was reacting; this person could give her the tools: 'How about trying this?'

Teachers and teaching

In her last year at her primary school, Sandy was taught by a male teacher who was very patient with her and to whom Sandy related well. Sandy respected him, even though they had some 'bust ups'. Her teaching assistant had worked with Sandy for about three years. She was very keen to improve her understanding and approaches with the children she supported, by doing various training courses, including the Thrive training and the Solihill parent training programme. She had become the school's Thrive practitioner and used what she had learned in her support work. Sandy's mother respected the assistant's work, but she had some reservations, given the complexity of Sandy's needs, about whether Sandy needed something different from what she was getting.

During her interview, Sandy described two of her teachers at her current residential school as 'annoying'. This was because she was not allowed out to do things like other children. However, Sandy did like the deputy head teacher because she felt listened to by her. She also liked the teaching assistants because they did not 'talk in your face constantly'. When she needs help from an assistant she calls her over and, unlike the teachers, they do not tell you what to do.

What helps/hinders learning

Sandy's mother believed that Sandy needed one-to-one teaching until she felt comfortable enough to learn by herself. She also believed that Sandy was now spending time in class at her current special school receiving more personal attention. While at primary school, Sandy's assistant had developed a range of strategies which she believed worked with Sandy; distract her to do something else for a short period and then return to the original task, building a bond of trust with her by treating each day as a fresh start, whatever happened the previous day, breaking the activity into small sections because of her short concentration span and having boundaries that were used consistently that made her feel safe. She also believed that Sandy worked best when she had minimal contact with other children, even though this was not appropriate for most children.

Sandy said that she preferred using a computer keyboard to writing by hand. Though she could not say what kind of teaching helped her learn, she was clear about what teaching annoyed her, such as being asked to do a piece of work again when it was not how the teacher wanted it done. She was also annoyed when she was given year 3 level maths when she was in year 7. However, she could explain what the deputy head did to help her; this was about helping her calm down and listening to her.

Placement

Sandy's mother felt that Sandy's stay at her primary school through to year 5 had 'run its course'. She felt that 'they did everything, but they didn't have the resources for it, they need the people to do it and she takes up everybody's time'. After her primary school Sandy spent some time at an alternative provision before going to a residential special school. This placement lasted for several months till she was sent home. Sandy's mother described how the school initially seemed to be the right place, but problems soon emerged. At a second special school placement there had been problems between Sandy's mother and staff over Sandy coming home over the holidays. Sandy was finally excluded for an incident and sent home without any prior notice.

Sandy's mother described how she had not considered special school for Sandy when she was younger as she wanted her to be in their local community. However, Sandy's mother recalled a psychologist who talked about secondary transition as a key period and began to wonder if Sandy would survive in the local secondary school. For her mother, Sandy did not 'quite grasp that she's supposed to work and toe the line like everyone else'. On the other hand, her mother felt 'bullied by it all', as she did not have many options.

Sandy's assistant explained that primary school staff felt they had failed Sandy because there was only a year to go before secondary transfer. Sandy became more aggressive, during a period when the assistant was ill, and attacked a member of staff. This is when special school became a serious prospect. As her assistant explained, 'we were just hoping that somebody out there would say – this child really does need some professional support other than education'. For Sandy's assistant, this was a sad situation: 'to me a child getting permanently excluded is not a way forward for anybody'. When Sandy was asked, she said that she preferred going to her residential school than to the local secondary school as her friends told her that it was 'rubbish'.

Sandy's mother had clear ideas about the kind of placement that she thought would benefit Sandy. She needed lots of exercise, stimulation and challenge. This was why she favoured a 'boot camp' approach. She realized that Sandy would 'probably hate it for a minute, but love it at the same time'. This might give Sandy the experiences that she had missed, despite the different clubs and activities that had been tried. The local area was described as having few outside school activities and the primary school also had few club activities. She felt that children learned much about themselves from teams, and Sandy had missed out on this. On the subject of inclusion, though Sandy's mother supported local schools and keeping children in their community, she recognized that 'nobody likes what they're doing all the time, do they?' She agreed that she now saw residential schools as appropriate for some children. For Sandy's assistant, she now looks back and considers it was 'wrong to hang on to' a child like Sandy. She explained that: 'if they've got the right type of provision then I think sometimes mainstream schools are not adequately suited for the Sandys of this world. And to have kept her so long in a mainstream school must have been a nightmare for her.'

Parental involvement

Sandy's mother described how she was often called into Sandy's primary school about incidents, such as running out of the school. Her mother was wanting a relationship with the school which helped her with Sandy. From her view, the school was 'always all right with me'. Sandy's assistant said that Sandy's mother and step-father were very supportive of Sandy at school. The assistant had contact with Sandy's mother most days to exchange information about how Sandy was getting on. They also used a home contact book to record what they wanted to exchange. Sandy's assistant also explained that there were no disagreements between her mother and the school staff. She attributed this to Sandy's mother knowing what Sandy was like at home; 'she dealt with her 24/7 . . . and she used to say to us, "How do you keep her in this school? I don't know."'

Sandy's mother explained that she did not always understand what went on in her own relationship with other professionals; 'they use all this lingo around you like you'd know, and you don't'. She also felt that she did not know what their roles were and what they could provide. When she reflected on her meetings with professionals she believed that 'we'd go from one year to the next year and we'd all be sat there again'.

Sandy's mother also discussed how she agreed to Sandy having a protection order which was organized by a social worker to make the case for Sandy to have residential support. It was at this stage that she received support from the Information and Advice Service. She was very appreciative of their support which managed to help get the process moving again. Sandy's mother was not a member or linked to any voluntary group or network, because, as she said, 'I haven't got time.'

Social interaction

Sandy's mother described Sandy as someone who most people would like at a first meeting. However, relationships were more fraught at home. Her relationship with her younger brother moved between being loving, but then pinching or bullying him. However, her brother missed her now she was away at school. Sandy's mother also described Sandy at home as 'overpowering'. The family was very short of space and was about to move to a larger flat. Despite her mother's attempts, Sandy did not communicate her feelings to her mother: 'She keeps it all in.' But Sandy did notice that her mother became upset about what was happening: 'She just thinks I'm moaning and being an idiot – "Just stop crying; stop crying mum."'

Sandy had no contact with her father, but as her step-father had known her since she was a 1-year-old, her mother felt that he was effectively her father. However, Sandy's assistant recalled how Sandy used to say that she wanted contact with her father. She once met her father and was heard to say that she did not like him and did not want anything to do with him.

When Sandy was interviewed at home she talked about the two girls, from her primary school, sitting in another room waiting for her. Sandy considered them to be her friends and she felt that they counted her as a friend too. She also felt that moving to a residential school had not affected her previous friendships adversely. Sandy's mother talked about how Sandy could sometimes be 'oblivious' of her friends' needs when they come to visit. At primary school Sandy was also described as struggling with her friends, Sandy's assistant confirmed. When Sandy was not present, other girls revealed that they were frightened of her: 'she'll terrorize us outside of school if we're not friends', as the assistant reported. Sandy was described as having 'power' in the classroom, something which Sandy knew she had. Many children kept their distance, while others would play with her because they were frightened not to. Yet, she was described as having one girl as a friend for quite a while. From her assistant's perspective, Sandy's behaviour was less an expression of deliberate bullying and more about having anger outbursts. Though other children had seen her behaviour in the classroom over the years, they accepted it because they had been with her since nursery and felt 'It's just Sandy.'

Future

Sandy's mother felt that she did not know what kind of future to expect for Sandy as these issues had persisted for so long. Her worries were about her 'just coping in life' and that she can be easily led. She worried that Sandy could do something 'really serious', because she liked to be the centre of attention. Her mother said: 'I want her to be all right in herself, at the end of the day . . . sod school, that's how I feel. And I really wish I'd pulled her out and not put us through it because I think it's destroyed us, relationship-wise'.

Sandy's assistant mentioned that Sandy's mother was worried about where Sandy will end up if the residential provision is not successful. The assistant worried that Sandy might self-harm. Underlying this, according to her assistant, was Sandy not 'knowing when to stop' and 'having no fear of anything', with the other risk that Sandy might also turn her aggression on to someone else. For her assistant, much of the future hangs on her current special school. By contrast, when Sandy was asked about any worries about the future, she replied no. But she saw her immediate future as carrying on at this residential school and realized that her mother wanted this too. However, Sandy did have clear ideas about what she wanted to do occupationally. She wanted to be a paramedic or a firewoman, though she could not explain why these jobs attracted her interest.

Sandy's mother would like Sandy to be at a school like her present one, but closer to home. She also did not want Sandy to be away from home till she was 18 years old. Her mother's view was that Sandy was 'intelligent enough' to do things for herself, as 'I did it. I didn't get much at school but I've learned a lot since, you know, and I'm self-taught.' Her expressed view about the current residential special school provision was 'I hope it's not too late.'

8

Tom

Mother: 'Don't let them grind you down – fight. Find out everything you can about the support that there is available and go for it, if you think your child could benefit. You have to really fight; if you just let it happen it won't happen. We wouldn't be where we are now at this school if I hadn't fought to get the Statement.'

Teacher: 'Take the time to get to know each other, the parents and the child – especially the child. It does take time and you need to make that time. Otherwise you're only going to be able to focus on one aspect and not see the bigger picture.'

Background information

Tom is 7 years old and in year 2 of an urban primary school which he attends because of its speech and language centre. He came to the school when he was 4 years old. He lives with his parents and younger brother, aged 3, just outside the urban area where he goes to school. Tom was interviewed at school, as was his teacher, the coordinator of the Centre. His mother was interviewed outside the school.

Identification

Strengths and difficulties

Tom's mother described him as a 'very lively, very sociable boy' and 'really happy little chap'. He is small for his age, about the height of a 4-year-old, and his speech sounds a 'little blurred'. Other than that his mother said that 'if you were looking at him, you wouldn't really know that there was anything wrong'. His teacher described Tom as 'determined, confident, outward and very communicative'.

Background health and early development

His mother described Tom as having had a lot of illness in his early years. He was born with the condition called tracheoesophageal fistula or TOF (his oesophagus did not form properly and instead it joined to his trachea, so when he was born he could not eat orally or breathe properly). Tom has been in various national medical centres for his condition and spent 11 months in these when he was born. He had been very ill at that stage, having had heart attacks, septicaemia and several life-threatening operations. As his mother explained, when 'he finally came home at eleven months he was basically a new born'. He could 'not do anything at all and he was gastrostomy fed from the day after he was born'. During one of the operations the vagus nerve in his stomach was damaged, the effect of which was that he has dumping syndrome. This means that he cannot have any sugary or fruit drinks or have a lot of sweet things, for which he has had drug treatment since he was very young. As his mother described, 'his health was his severest difficulty and he didn't walk until he was over two; he was at physiotherapy and occupational therapy . . . you name it, he had it'.

Fairly soon after Tom came out of hospital he attended a specialist centre where it became clear that his speech was affected. He had some speech and language therapy there, but only for short periods. At the time his mother thought these difficulties were due to his long hospital stay, but now the professionals see the difficulties as unrelated to his hospital stay. Tom has communicated through Makaton signs from 2 years old. At that time Tom made no comprehensible speech sounds; nor did he eat orally. He had a gastrostomy peg (a surgical opening through the abdomen into the stomach; a feeding device is inserted through this opening to feed the child directly into their stomach, so bypassing the mouth and throat). The Makaton signing, as his mother put it: 'just changed our lives, and it meant I could understand him a bit better and communicate with him a bit more, and he could tell me his needs'.

Tom attended the specialist centre for some time while he went in and out of hospital because, as his mother explained, he caught various illnesses and was 'very vulnerable'. He has had two heart operations and has had a catheter fitted quite recently. His mother described how this operation 'changed his life; he's got so much more energy now and he doesn't keep telling me he's out of air'.

After the specialist centre Tom then went to a nursery which specialized in speech and language for pre-school children. There he had formal speech therapy twice a week and started to make progress with his speech. But, in addition to his speech difficulties, Tom has had a divergent squint which is ongoing. He tends to look in different directions with his eyes and so might miss something on the floor right next to him. He has also had a mid-line crossover impairment (bringing an arm or leg across the line to the other side of the body; it is usually an indication of poor balance and coordination difficulties). The crossover capability is a developmental phase that children go through when they are very young. In Tom's case these difficulties affected his handwriting and balancing, as his teacher explained. To address these difficulties Tom does the Fun Fit programme (designed to enhance motor coordination skills and activities).

It was at this stage that his parents heard about the speech and language centre at the primary school where he is now. They met the centre coordinator who then began to liaise with them about whether Tom met the criteria for entry to the centre. Tom's teacher, who was the coordinator and first saw him in the pre-school nursery, she described how they had to establish whether Tom's speech difficulty 'was as a result of or related to any of the other areas of needs that he had'. There are criteria for entry to the centre that the children's language or a speech difficulty cannot be attributed to another area of need'. The issues about this matter are discussed below.

Tom's teacher described Tom as almost 'completely non-verbal' when he started at the centre, but he did sign using Makaton. His mother described how he has done 'remarkably well' considering where he started. She described how his teachers report that Tom is average for his age, or just below average in most subjects. Maths was described as at a 'relatively good level', while 'his expressive language was below average. She also explained that from her perspective she was also interested in whether Tom can read his book to her and get to bed on time. She explained that the children she can compare him with are those that go to the Beavers (the young scouts group) and 'they seem to be massively farther ahead than him'. But, she noticed that his behaviour was changing: 'he doesn't grab as much now as he used to because he can speak'. But she also now noticed how quickly Tom's younger brother was developing, and this made her realize 'how severe the damage was to Tom in the early years'.

Tom's teacher described Tom as a 'bright boy' who was at an age-appropriate attainment level in all areas. She also talked about 'concerns over his physical development because of the medical needs'; he does not have the 'muscle strength that you would expect for a child of that age'. She did point out, however, that though his early difficulties could have adversely affected his literacy, this was not the case. Though his mother had expressed concerns about Tom's spelling, his attainments in spelling were also average for his age. His teacher also noted that Tom's expressive language was lower at the word level than his other language, according to the speech therapist assessment. She suggested that this may be due to his 'medical background and being in hospital for a long time.

Tom, in his interview, said that things at school were 'good' for him. Though he liked others reading stories to him, he found reading 'complicated'. He said that he preferred writing to reading and he felt he was 'good at writing' as well as maths and literacy.

Diagnosis and implications

Tom's teacher described how Tom was identified when he came to the centre as having verbal dyspraxia (a difficulty in making and coordinating the precise movements needed to produce clear speech; and without any signs of damage to nerves or muscles). She compared him with another child who started at the centre at the same time who had similar verbal dyspraxic difficulties, but not the same medical background. The two boys presented differently; Tom as confident, sociable and outgoing and keen to get his message across, while the other boy was passive, withdrawn and a reluctant communicator. She also mentioned that Tom was well supported at home and had been to a pre-school setting that was engaged with his needs, so he came with the expectation that he would be understood and he would participate'.

Tom's teacher believed that he was aware of some of his expressive difficulties, but he had learned to correct himself when prompted. She also thought that his awareness did 'not bother him; he's a very confident resilient child'. Tom's mother also described some of his frustrations with speaking, but she felt that now that the school had 'done such an amazing job with him, his confidence levels are a lot stronger'. But, she felt that he was still 'vulnerable; if anything little happens he bursts into tears very quickly'.

The impact of Tom's condition on his parents was described by his mother as 'incomprehensibly stressful from the start' and that it remains so when they have to prepare reviews, transition to other schools or his many paediatric appointments. One of her current concerns was whether they are 'doing the right thing taking him away from the school (where) he's happy'. She also talked about the many medical appointments with different professionals that Tom had to attend to monitor his various treatments. She then described how Tom's younger brother was unaware of Tom's difficulties, but that it is hard for him; as she explained, 'I don't get the time that I want to spend with him; he has to come around with me to all the appointments.' She also spends much time with Tom, doing his speech exercises, and he takes a long time to eat, have a bath and do his homework. However, she does have time with his younger brother when Tom is at school.

Tom's teacher talked about how life for his parents 'hasn't been plain sailing', given the complexity of his special educational needs. She described how 'at any level it is hard, but when you've got so many different factors to understand how they fit together', it is really hard. She also appreciated that it was doubly hard for his parents because of the uncertainties in the changing SEN system and the procedures required to access the specialist centre at his current school. She described these procedures as a 'bit of a minefield as to how to apply for a place, how to get a place, what information needed to be sought and shared and discussed'.

Labels and others' reactions

Tom's teacher identified his special educational needs as in the area of speech, language and communication needs. She identified his specific difficulties as about speech, and saw no specific language difficulties involved. Tom's mother thought that others would at first meeting see Tom as 'very small' and perhaps think he was 4 years old, unless he spoke to them. Then they might hear him struggle a little to understand what he was saying. She also described his eyes as different, but did not see that as very significant. However, other children's response to him has been variable. When he first started at this school he was called 'baby'. Some children would want to mother him and smother him. Because he could not speak then, his way of getting attention was to grab people.

There were also other episodes which upset her. His mother described how, when Tom was gastrostomy fed and had breathing difficulties, people would stare at them when they were in public. She was told not to take her child out when he was throwing up, which occurred several times a day due to severe reflux. Some people would cross the road because of his breathing sounds. She gave another example of when he went to a Halloween dance, when he had been at the school for a few months. Other children laughed at him and ignored him. His mother then took him home crying: 'he was very sad and I was really upset'. The school were very supportive.

At that time Tom had little speech, but since then this kind of reaction has changed. The other children have become older and they have 'grown up together . . . he's now just one of the team'. His mother felt that 'he seems to be really happy and he always seems to have a lot of friends that he talks to me about'. She felt that 'they all seem to accept him and he's just Tom now, which is fantastic'. Tom's teacher thought that he did not conceal his speech difficulties and discussed how other children responded to him positively, given the 'positive ethos and principles' in the school.

Statement/Plan

Tom was issued with a Statement when he was about 2 years old. For his mother, the whole experience of securing a Statement was described as having been 'hell'. At that stage Tom was gastrostomy fed, he could not walk or talk, nor eat orally. His mother applied for a Statement to get some funding for him at pre-school as assistance was needed with feeding him. She initially approached the Portage worker about getting a Statement, but was told she would not get one because she had 'bullied' the key worker into making her apply for a Statement. As a result, his mother approached the head of the Portage service again. Tom's mother described herself as 'being just hysterical and so stressed about what to do and the utter lack of support'. This person dealt with it positively, and after a great deal of extra work for his parents and the team around him they agreed to issue a Statement.

But Tom's mother also described how she felt that she was struggling at home at that stage with the 'constant feeding four times a day, and he was sick every time he had food'. She could not leave the house, and her husband came home late from work. She needed help, and when someone told her about a fund for carers, she applied and received some funds. She was then told that her funding was to be cut because she did not need it. At that stage the Statement had still not been issued. The 'frustrating thing' for Tom's mother was that 'nobody told you anything . . . you had to find everything out yourself'.

But, when Tom was issued with a Statement there was initially no funding attached to the Statement because he was not at school. Tom's mother also recalled that she was then dealing with someone who was very supportive. But this person moved on, as part of a constant turnover of authority staff. However, as regards the funding for Tom at pre-school, there were some early years funds that the pre-school received directly, that were not connected to the Statement. They hired someone to feed Tom, give him his medication, and introduce Makaton to aid his communication. For his mother, the pre-school was 'utterly amazing' and 'turned it all around, and took Makaton to their hearts', explaining that she actually trained them in Makaton.

Tom's mother also explained that Tom's Statement has itself not been changed since it was issued, though there have been annual reviews which record changes in his needs. Tom was going to continue with a Statement when he moves to the primary school, but there will be no funding attached to the Statement. Nor was Tom's Statement to be transferred to an EHC Plan till he was in year 5.

For Tom's mother a Statement was 'definitely necessary' because 'without it he wouldn't be where he is'. But she was also doubtful of the value of its specific content. She thought that what mattered was that 'he's getting the best that he possibly can'. This was why 'it's important to have (the Statement) as a backup'. She had at some stage thought that she might have to use the Statement's legal status to enforce what was needed for him. This was when she was fighting for speech therapy and transport for him. She recognized that she had been 'very lucky' because many other parents have had to fight for provision.

Learning: what and how

Provision

Tom's mother discussed how he currently receives speech therapy support twice a week and that he also has an additional physical education programme (Fun Fit). She recognized that the school thought that he needed less therapy this year than last, and also that it was disruptive for him to have time out of class. So he has the extra sessions outside class time. Tom has a key worker who is a teaching assistant he shares with another boy in the same class who also has some speech difficulties. Tom's mother, when talking about his progress since he started at the school, said that she has 'only got praise for the school'. She also explained that the centre's speech therapist would initially provide support when he starts at his new primary school and that there was community-based therapy to support Tom as needs be.

Tom himself was able to talk about the extra lessons he has to help him 'say things'. He described having these with his friend and that the two of them played games in the lessons. He felt that this had helped him and that he went less often now than last year, because he and his friend were 'too clever'.

His teacher gave a fuller account of his additional provision since he started at the school. The provision aimed to develop his speech and language and give him more confidence to communicate with others. The centre teaching assistant was described by his teacher as the lynchpin for connecting the centre to the classroom. She is in that class four days a week, while there is also a mainstream assistant in Tom's class part time. The centre assistant also sits in while the therapist works with Tom, and then she will run the programme at other times with him. The class teacher also has the opportunity to sit in during the therapy sessions. So Tom has three to four therapy sessions per week, and also accesses Fun Fit and a programme overseen by the occupational therapist to strengthen his core muscle strength and his fine motor skills.

When Tom relied more on Makaton signing the approach was to have him in a group of about six children who learned to extend their signing as part of the social use of language in a practical and fun way. This signing was taken back to the whole class where the teacher and assistant used it with everyone in class. Signing was used with various class activities, e.g. when viewing a DVD and at class assemblies. Tom's teacher mentioned that they had positive feedback from 'all parents, particularly children for whom English was an additional language (EAL)', about the signing. Currently Tom's additional speech therapy provision focused on words from the curriculum and ones he struggled with at home – for example, clapping out syllables and chanting words. His teacher believed that his future provision will continue to need to focus on the pre-teaching of vocabulary and multi-syllabic words to give him time to learn these before accessing them in the lesson.

Tom's teacher summarized the school approach with its centre as inclusive, which meant the children were in class full time, but the children with speech and language difficulties are not just 'dropped in' to see if they 'sink or swim'. They are as flexible as possible and 'adapt everything that we need to adapt'. Tom has access to a differentiated curriculum, as would anybody else, and he has speech therapy sessions. The centre also organizes regular 'team around the child' meetings, with all involved, to agree on the child's current strengths and difficulties and what needs to be 'put into place'. There is an 'All about me' passport which Tom contributes to, and a speech and language therapy/centre annual report which they go through with the class teacher and assistants.

Learning progress

Tom talked during his interview about how his teacher helped him learn, and also that he completes his work quickly: 'I normally finish second or third, but never finish last.' He talked proudly about how he had learned to 'say everything now', but how sometimes he does not get it right first time, but does when he tries a second time. However, he recognized that there were still some 'words I don't get'. Tom also talked about his learning maths and said at first that learning maths was more important than speaking, but later admitted that 'actually both of them are more or less the same'. He also mentioned that he and his friend 'know a lot of signing', but that they do not use it 'much any more 'cos I know my words'. Tom's teacher explained that his progress had been such that he no longer needed the support he had in the past, which was why they were planning to 'transfer him out of the centre a year early' (other pupils stay in the centre mostly for an extra year). For his mother, Tom had 'made phenomenal progress'.

Teachers and teaching assistants

Tom's mother discussed how Tom got on very well with his teachers and assistants. Everyone at the school had said that they did not want him to leave the school; that 'he charms them' and is a 'pleasure to work with'. Tom himself said he got on well and he 'never' had arguments. Tom's mother felt that Tom's assistant has been a 'rock' for him; she had previously been a paediatric nurse, so she understands some of the issues. Tom also had a mealtime assistant, which he no longer needed. He goes to lunch first as his eating is slow because swallowing is hard for him. Tom spoke about his two assistants and talked about the centre assistant as 'fantastic'. But he refused to accept that this assistant helped him learn, because 'I'm too clever.' Tom's teacher talked about the training and supervision of the centre assistants. They all do the local authority organized training by the specialist advisory teachers and, in addition, do in-house training with the centre coordinator and therapist. Assistants also video some of their sessions with children, and they jointly review them with the therapist.

What helps/hinders learning

Tom's mother discussed how Tom likes interactive learning, especially using computers – for example, ones which are maths-based and involve games. She talked about him as being energetic, but that he can become easily distracted. For instance, while his brother can watch a whole film, Tom would watch for five to ten minutes, and then become bored. She believed he struggled with activities that involved higher concentration levels. Tom's teacher endorsed what his mother said about Tom responding to what he finds enjoyable. She added that he learns when he sees the relevance of what he is doing and when it builds on 'things that he's good at' and 'it's an appropriate challenge'. She also thought that the support he had been having helped him learn, whether 'talking to a friend, checking it with them, or using the prompt sheets that are there'. His teacher also identified something about Tom's personal style which can sometimes hinder his learning. Tom likes to communicate and lead, and she felt that this needed to be 'reined in' to ensure that he listens to others.

Placement

Getting to his current school

Tom's mother explained how he came to be at this primary school because of the speech and language centre. As described above, Tom was at a pre-school in a part of an urban area where his family lived. The family moved to a more rural village and then looked for a primary school there. Tom's mother did not know then about the current school with its centre. Tom was at that stage gastrostomy fed, and the school said that they could not accept Tom because they could not deal with this situation. For his mother it was 'really hard to hear that there was a school that could help him, but they weren't prepared to'. So she 'fought as hard as (she) possibly could' by contacting everybody involved with Tom to have a Statement review. The centre coordinator came to this review with all the others involved. Subsequently, when she contacted the local authority they agreed that the school was appropriate for Tom, influenced by the report from the pre-school setting. Tom's mother recalled one of the quotes from this report which said that 'they've had lots of children who could talk but chose not to, but they've never had a child who wanted to talk so much, but couldn't as Tom'. Tom was also beginning then to be weaned off the gastrostomy feed, which he was off fully before he started at this primary school, having to resort back only when he was very ill.

Tom's mother appreciated that it was probably very daunting for this school to take on Tom as they might have felt that this was something they 'just can't do'. She was also pleased that the coordinator was 'cautious, as I wouldn't want anybody's child being detrimentally affected by a new child coming in'.

Change of school

As discussed above, Tom is due to go to a primary school nearer where the family live next school year, where he will be going into year 3 at the same time his 3-year-old younger brother starts at reception in the same school. The head teacher and SEN coordinator of the new school support this move, and the local authority are in agreement too. His mother discussed how, at first, Tom was very excited about the move, but as it dawned on him that he will not be with his two friends, he started to say that he wanted to stay for another year. Tom himself said in his interview that he was going to this new school with his brother. When asked to explain why this was happening, he said that he needed to 'move on', and that the reason was because 'I'm too clever.' But he felt it was 'bad' as he had more friends at his current school and, as he said, 'I really love it and I do not want to leave.' He said, however, that they would come to his party and that he knew some of the children at the new school from the Beavers.

For Tom's teacher, despite the reservations about Tom leaving his current school, she believed it would be a 'disservice if we didn't put him forward to go back to his local mainstream'. Tom would have less travelling to his new local school and this was a factor, given that he does 'tire a lot more easily than other children'. She saw his parents as seeing that 'the benefits outweighed the drawbacks'.

Inclusion/exclusion

Tom's mother believed that having a centre at the school was 'brilliant', as he was 'in a mainstream environment learning with others who had no difficulties'. Tom was then able to 'go away from it and come back again . . . it is just perfect'. She did add that 'it would have been ideal if it was at my local school'. But she realized that the centre was not that far from where they lived, especially as in that local authority there were few such centres, expressing that, 'I'm really lucky it's that close really.'

His mother also believed in having 'children with disabilities in the class who can cope; if it's not going to be too disruptive for everybody else'. But she qualified this by saying that 'obviously there are times when it's not possible, and the children do have to be in separate schools'. This, she believed, was relevant to some children with behavioural difficulties.

Tom's teacher considered that it was an 'anomaly' that the local authority had many more ordinary school-based resource bases for children with autism than with speech and language difficulties. It means that children with speech and language difficulties have longer distances to travel. Though she did realize that having an enhanced advisory and support service might enable more pupils to be in their local schools, she believed that the centre offered a kind of 'in-reach', where other schools could 'see good practice being done routinely'. This, she felt, helped to train others. But, she did believe that what was provided could be seen as 'almost like a token gesture, if I'm being brutally honest', and she also realized that 'the children that they get tend to be from the parents who have pushed and driven for that specialist provision'. But she still believed that there is a need for a place for 'skilling up other staff in the school and out of school'. For her, 'if we're going to have the capacity to have a fully inclusive education system, then more training needs to be put in place'.

Parental involvement

Get on with teachers and other professionals

Tom's mother was very pleased with the communications between the teachers and herself. There is a regular newsletter and a home–school communication book, which she uses very often. She felt that the school communicated back almost every day, and that this was above and beyond what they should be doing. She felt that she could 'go up and see the school at any time I want to'. Tom's teacher described their relationship with his mother as very positive, and that his mother's relationship with her was more informal than with his class teacher.

Tom's teacher also described how his mother would come to the school every week, when he first started, to talk about her concerns and go through things with 'a fine-tooth comb'. His teacher attributed this to her 'previous experience of having to fight for everything'. His teacher's approach was to find ways for her to 'feel confident in what we were doing'. However, at the start of this year Tom's therapist believed that he no longer needed direct therapy, and that his needs could be met in class. Tom's mother felt he still needed direct therapy and, as the therapist had the capacity, they decided to continue with it. Tom's teacher also felt that his mother still holds on to some of the negative feelings from her previous bad experiences.

Support groups

Tom's mother has been a member of a charitable group in which parents of children with special educational needs support other parents of children with special educational needs. When Tom came home from his initial stay in hospital, his mother did not have anyone to talk to. She found out about the group and met a befriender, who also had a child with TOF, who gave her support. Having benefited from this scheme she then trained to be a befriender and is available for other parents who need support in the same way she did.

Tom's mother has also had contact with the local Information and Advisory Service, which she described as having been 'fantastic'. They have helped her writing up forms to secure funding, and also in writing her views as part of the assessment for the Statement.

Social interaction

Tom's mother described him as very popular with his class, but that he did not socialize much outside of school because his school friends lived far away.

The key factor is his distance from the area of the school. But Tom does see children where he lives by going weekly to the Beavers group. His teacher talked about how some of the children when he started at his current school wanted to 'mother him'. She wondered if there might be a similar tendency when he starts at his new school.

Tom's mother talked about Tom's good friend, the other boy with speech difficulties at the centre. Because he lives quite far from where Tom lives, they do not see each other much outside school. It is difficult to arrange seeing him as, during weekdays and at weekends, Tom is involved in family activities. However, during the school holidays, Tom has spent time with some of his friends, and for his birthday had many children come to his party. When Tom talked about his friends, he made particular reference to two: the boy in the centre with him, and a girl. He mentioned that he saw them in the summer holidays. But he also talked about everyone in his class as being his friend, though he also gave a full account of an argument he had had over the distribution of glue sticks in class.

Tom's teacher confirmed that Tom was 'very accepted and liked', though he can sometimes be a 'little bit in your face'. She understood this in terms of when he was younger: 'the only way he could get attention was by tapping somebody'. He is now reminded that this is no longer appropriate. She also described him as very keen to get his message across, which has called for the staff to remind him to be patient, a message which he has been responsive to. His teacher also talked about how, despite him gravitating to his two close friends, he interacts well in class with other children. She thought that some kind of buddying scheme with another child would help his transition to the new school.

Tom's mother said that Tom's relationship with his brother was like most brothers; 'they love each other and play together, but they fight with each other'. His younger brother is more physical than Tom, who she had 'protected' because of his history. Tom also talked about 'always fighting' with his brother.

Future

Hopes and worries

Tom's mother said that she was hopeful that 'he will be able to progress as a normal mainstream child one day'. She did feel that he 'will achieve and do well so long as he's given the opportunities and the expectations are appropriate'. But she knew that he may always have some physical difficulties, and that 'he'll never be able to do some of the things that other people may choose not to do'. However, she was terrified about 'not knowing whether they will be able to support his needs' at the new school. But her contacts with the head teacher and the SEN coordinator there have given her some confidence. The head teacher has been straight with her about this; she did not say 'It'll be fine. Don't worry, it'll be great.' She has been 'honest', saying 'we will do our best, and there have been children that we haven't been able to accommodate.'

Tom's mother said that she knew it sounded silly, but she was also 'terrified' about Tom being small, red haired, not able to focus his eyes, and 'not able to speak properly'. Her concerns were about him being bullied. As she put it, 'my biggest fear is that he's not going to be happy and he's so happy here; I just don't know as a parent if I'm doing the right thing to take him out and bring him to his local school'. But she realized that it had to happen at some stage. From her perspective, opportunities for Tom needed to be embraced, even if 'it's going to be hard'. Tom's teacher understood his mother's emotions and concerns about Tom, saying it can be hard to tell parents about containing their anxiety.

Longer-term future

Tom was able to talk easily about going to the new school. He said that he did not know what he would be doing there, but did know that there is 'definitely no speech and language (therapy)'. His teacher saw a bright future for Tom. His mother saw him going to an ordinary secondary school where they will not put too much pressure on him.

9
Alex

Mother: 'Be patient with the child because it can take time. I mean Alex can't be rushed. And it isn't always easy to be patient. And for the teachers, I would say preparation more than anything and to not surprise them. In Alex's case, never make a change without preparing for it'.

Teaching assistant: 'Just because you've been on a course that said "This is what you need to do with a child with autism . . . this is how they learn", it's not set in stone. They're all different. And also, each day could be different. Be flexible. Ask for help if you're not sure.'

'And sit back as much as you can. Don't let them flounder, don't let them flounder at something . . . see what he can achieve before you go in and tell him what to do and how to do it. Because I think they can sometimes achieve more than they're allowed to do.'

Background information

Alex lived with his parents and went to a local urban primary school. He was 9, almost 10 years old, in year 5, and an only child. He was interviewed at school, as was his teaching assistant. His mother was interviewed outside school.

Identification

Strengths and difficulties

Alex's mother described him as 'very happy at the moment', even though he 'still finds a lot of things frustrating and he does still have anxieties'. She contrasted this with how he was when younger. He then experienced more anxieties and stress 'about what was happening around and things he didn't understand'. She also explained that Alex 'doesn't know he's any different to anyone else, although he obviously thinks differently to a lot of people, he has different interests to a lot of his peers'. When I asked Alex to say what he is like, he described himself as a 'good boy'. When asked if he found anything hard to do, he said that there was nothing, even when asked again in a different way.

His mother described how they had Alex assessed when he was younger for communication difficulties, because he 'never really played in a conventional sense'. He had been given many toys as gifts, but he never touched them. Instead of pushing trains, for example, he would spend much time spinning the wheels. Alex also used to collect jar lids and would spend time spinning them on the floor. At that stage Alex was still not talking and, as his mother put it, 'he used to scream at me a lot because he couldn't talk'. She described how he would roll on the floor and 'do the whole toddler tantrum until he was six or seven because everything would over-whelm him'. For example, if they tried taking him to a café, he could 'be on the floor rolling around'. For her, 'as a parent, you feel everyone's looking at you'. So they could not take him places 'without him getting very upset and getting very anxious'.

Alex no longer screams though he does a low-level 'groaning voice' when he is frustrated. He started sucking his fingers when he was a baby, which she saw as a way of soothing himself. This helped him go to sleep, so they did not discourage this. She realized that this is to be discouraged, as Alex's dentist does, but she felt that Alex 'needs to be able to calm himself'. She also described how when he becomes 'a bit panicky', he just wants 'a cuddle and he wants to be reassured'. She added that although 'you still can't really reason with him, he's more kind of accepting about difficult situations now'. However, when he experiences a change of situation, they need to plan so that he knows what is going to happen. She gave as an example, how they were going to a wedding over the weekend where he will meet people he does not know. So she is showing him pictures to become familiar with people and places.

She also described how he had become more sociable, but 'he's still happiest on his own'. So he does come and sit with his parents at home more than he used to do and shows them what he has drawn. But, as she explained, 'he never really wants to say "Oh, can I go to so and so for tea?" or "Can I have somebody home?"' He is much happier playing with paper 'that he can shape into butterflies'. His main interests 'revolve around flight – everything he's interested in can fly in some way or another'. This started with flying insects, so he was interested in butterflies and bees. This has been extended to birds, particularly gulls. He can identify different kinds of gulls as well as certain dragonflies, butterflies and birds; he can identify some birds through birdsong as well. In the autumn he becomes interested in the leaves falling from the trees because 'to him they fly'. He is also interested in fish because of how they 'fly through water'. So he is also very interested in aeroplanes. He has been to an air show, which he really enjoyed, and he likes watching planes fly into the nearby airport.

Other aspects of development and learning

Alex's first word was 'bee' in sight of a toy bee. Previously he had not babbled and did not 'make any effort to talk as such until he was about three'. His mother dated his interest in flying things since that age. She also described how he started to draw when he was about 6 years old, with one of the first drawings being a flying ladybird. He started to write a year later, which really frustrated him. She thought that he was now very good at spelling and had heard that some children in class, realizing this, had started to ask him to help with their spelling. For her, this was 'quite nice to have a bit of a mutual exchange where he actually gets more involved'. Alex himself said he was 'excellent' at maths and literacy. But his mother described him as having difficulties with several subjects, such as maths and reading comprehension, given his literal approach. However, she felt that he has been making progress' and was 'keeping up'.

His mother also described how Alex 'picked up certain things' such as phonics when he was younger. So, he learned to read much quicker than she expected. But although he can read fluently, 'how much he understands is another matter'. He is in the lower literacy group 'because he couldn't always understand what he read'. Though he can sometimes find what he reads funny, he does not always 'interpret things correctly'. Trying to explain idioms and phrases can be quite tricky, as are words that have the same spelling but different meanings. She also described how Alex responds in terms of not always picking up all the information he is given, not recalling what he has been asked to do, and not being able to filter out and concentrate on what he needs to do.

Alex's mother was pleased that they have no longer had any difficulties in getting him into school since he started year 5. Though Alex might say now that he did not want to go 'he doesn't actually create and get really upset'. His teaching assistant confirmed this improvement when she described how 'behaviourally we don't experience any problems'. However, at times he becomes stressed: 'he'll ruffle his hair and he tends to go red in the face and look as though he's about to cry, but doesn't'.

Alex's assistant described how he struggled academically, his attainments being 'behind his peers, and the gap is growing'. Despite this, he has made progress in maths over the last year. He continues to struggle to solve maths problems 'straight off' without someone going back and prompting him to consider what he knows and has done before. When he was in year 3, two years ago, he could hardly write his name, while now he 'quite happily writes two or three pages', and he can punctuate. His assistant also commented on how Alex could become 'obsessed' with some of the structured language procedures they teach – for example, for possessive phrases. Alex links on to something like this and tries to use it all the time, even when inappropriately.

Alex's assistant confirmed what his mother said about his reading accuracy. But she also commented that those in his reading group are improving their comprehension faster than he has been. She remarked about how he struggled with feelings, but felt that she knew him long enough to 'know when there's something up, even though he can't necessarily tell me what it is'. She concluded that, given what he was like when he was younger, 'we'd say he's grown up and matured'.

Diagnosis and implications

Alex's parents became aware of this problems by comparison with his mother's nephew of a similar age, who talked to them about books that he read and would ask them questions. Alex played with the same toy over and over again and would 'blank everyone in the room completely'. His mother described how she became more aware of his difficulties and their significance when he went to a pre-school playgroup. Another woman had noticed how Alex reacted to a biscuit at break time; instead of eating it, he would spin it and become upset if the biscuit broke. She asked his mother whether she had considered autism and gave her a book to read about it. Alex's mother realized that Alex did not present the 'classic' picture of autism as he had good eye contact and wanted to be cuddled, but there was the spinning, and Alex did not like being with other children: 'he didn't enjoy toddler groups really'.

Alex's mother took him to see the health visitor when he was about 2-years-old about him not standing, walking or talking. Following a period of several weeks of assessment, Alex was given the autistic spectrum disorder diagnosis when he was 3 years old. The effect on his mother was to wonder whether 'it's something you've done, as a mum'. She also wondered if she 'could have done something differently when he was born'. But, she often considers that 'it must be genetic or there's some kind of genetic element', because she has observed autism running in some families.

For Alex's assistant his autism was shown in his struggling with social interaction. She described how Alex often says 'he hasn't got any friends'. At school they have tried to steer him towards activities with other children, particularly at lunchtimes. The other element is his 'occasional literal use of language'. She described how she has to 'be really careful what I say to him and how I say things, but sometimes I do forget'. But, she added, he did not show much repetitive use of language.

Alex's mother discussed how she and her husband have not told Alex about the diagnosis. This was because he has not asked about it and 'he's never seemed to be unhappy about the way things are'. She explained that they had decided that if the time came when he was unhappy about being supported at school, that would be when they they would say 'this is why you're supported'. She mentioned that Alex has 'never really questioned that he's different . . . never really been concerned that he thinks differently'. She realized that, compared to other children with an autism diagnosis who know about it, Alex has been treated differently.

Alex's mother described the initial impact of his condition on her. At the time she felt 'Is this it? Is he just going to scream at us for the rest of his life? Is that what it means?' At that time this was all they had experienced: 'it did make a difference obviously, and it did feel quite devastating in a way because we didn't know what we were going to be faced with, how he was going to manage, how we were going to manage looking after him, was he ever going to be independent, was he ever going to be able to look after himself?' It also made them decide to have no more children, 'because we didn't know what we were going to be faced with and how we'd manage with him and other children'. She also explained that she was conscious of him 'being different when he was younger because of his behaviour'. She said that it was not so much being embarrassed about the behaviour as anxious for him and how she could support him.

Labels and others' reactions

Alex's mother said that the diagnosis had been 'autistic spectrum disorder', and that was the term she used rather than 'autistic spectrum condition', which she noticed others were now using. For her, 'Alex has autism', seemed to apply. The label 'helped us understand the way he was and gave us a bit of an insight in to why he was, (I don't want to say) different'. His assistant explained that, from her experience, Alex was not aware of his condition, though she said that he is 'becoming aware that he always has to sit with me, and he has a designated lunchtime support mealtime assistant'. Nobody at school said anything to him about it as the 'children have always known him having somebody helping him . . . they are very good and understanding'.

Alex's mother also discussed how she might explain to somebody who observed one of his 'complete meltdowns'. She gave, as an example, an occasion when he was refusing to get on to a bus and somebody was watching and staring at him. His mother said 'I'm sorry, he's got autism', and the man said 'Yes. So has my grandson.' This has happened in other situations too, so it is something 'that people are more familiar with'.

His mother discussed how her parents found it difficult at times to cope with Alex. Though they do not see them often, given where they live, they compare him with their other grandchildren. Alex has a different outlook from his cousins, and is not interested in bikes and scooters. His mother felt that it was not something her parents did deliberately; they were just not familiar with the way he was. She thought that they have gradually become 'more aware of how he was and that he has his own interests'. It helped when Alex started liking aeroplanes because her father always liked aeroplanes, so they had a common interest to talk about.

The school had never said that he cannot go on a school trip, but there was an issue about whether he could stay overnight during a school trip. His mother wondered if he could manage it and who would support him. She was also not sure if Alex would want to go as he has never been away overnight from his parents. She knew that there were other children who also do not want to go. She realized that 'it feels like it's not an inclusive thing, but then mainstream schools aren't – they do their best'.

Statement/Plan

Alex had a Statement from the time he started at school at 4 years old, though for the initial period his mother went into school to support him till the support staff arrangements started. The Statement refers specifically to his assistant support (as 0.8 full time), but as his mother noted it is quite 'vague' as regards his teaching programme. He is due to have the Statement transferred into an EHC Plan, but in the authority there is some delay in this transfer process. His mother also mentioned that, in that authority, there was also some discussion of whether all Statements were to be converted into Plans, as the authority was trying to reduce the number of Statements/Plans. However, from his assistant's perspective, she saw any transfer as resulting in the same level of support as he now receives. Overall, Alex's mother felt the process had been 'fairly smooth', and that with his annual reviews and his IEPs they have had confidence that they can meet his needs. In her view this was the 'best thing for him' as they recognized his needs from an early stage.

Learning: what and how

Provision

His mother said that Alex's provision suited him because he was making progress. In class he is in a group as part of a class-wide system where children are organized into literacy and maths groups of a range of abilities, as his assistant explained. Alex tends to work mainly with his assistant, though 'sometimes he gets a little bit frustrated that it's always me and not a friend or a peer'. His mother and assistant talked about him having extra teaching in maths lessons, but he did not like missing assembly for these lessons, according to his mother. His mother also talked about Alex being aware that he has an 'adult buddy', when the other children had their peers as buddies when the buddy system operated. Over the last two years he has not been withdrawn from class by his assistant, as he had been in the previous year, as 'he doesn't want to be apart from everyone else – he wants to be with everyone else'.

Alex's mother discussed how, when they do various projects in class – for example, the Stuarts and the Great Fire of London – he can find something that interests him. He tends to 'latch on to a certain extent'. Recently it was The Plague, while he was not bothered by the rest of the Stuart period. She described how he also likes French, so she concluded that 'he does seem to be engaged in most things'. However, she noticed that they do less for him now than they used to when he was in the infants, so that he can become more independent. But, they do provide him with visual prompts to help him to remember to do various tasks in class – for example, to unpack his bag, and other activities at various points in the day. She also noted how when they wanted to change his literacy group, he could not cope with this, so they let him stay in the same group. She realized that there was a balance to strike between providing what he needs and 'allowing him to manage himself when he can'.

His mother said that she and her husband had not 'really pushed him academically', but they do support him 'because to a certain extent he's got to manage the best he can'. She felt that Alex 'can only do what he can do . . . he probably has got learning difficulties, but he's managing to the best of his ability'. She also described how Alex was willing to do his homework, though in his own way.

During his interview Alex talked about doing some multiplying of numbers using the 2 by 2 grid method that morning, which he said he could do by himself. He also talked about liking French, biology and RE. Alex also talked about his assistant helping him with literacy and maths. It was clear that Alex liked coming to school, saying that 'I'm happy at my school.'

His assistant described how she supports him all week except for two after-noons, one of which she teaches the whole class, including him. For maths and lit-eracy he is part of a small group (five to seven children) with a range of attainments, with some children needing less support than Alex. In her view, Alex can access the same curriculum goals as the rest of the class with the level of support he gets. His assistant was present during his interview, and when she asked him what she does to help him, he said 'write down the answers'. His assistant firmly denied this saying that she 'makes sure you're listening, don't I?' She also explained how, during whole-class learning time, she and Alex sit on chairs while the rest of the class sit on the carpet: 'you can't sit on the carpet because I'm your partner and I'm too old to sit on the carpet!' Alex then said, 'when you're not here I can sit on the carpet'.

Adaptations and what is worth learning

Both Alex's mother and his assistant believed that he needed the same broad kind of curriculum as other children. His mother recognized that he needed more maths teaching, but he was not the only one in the class struggling with maths. She also thought it was important for him to learn how to cope with people, especially as he gets older. She saw this as important for all children, not just someone like Alex.

His assistant did not see herself as supporting him in an 'overly specialized way': 'I see what we're doing as just slightly modifying to accommodate.' She saw this as an 'extension and not as a serious modification'. She also discussed how they are addressing the social aspects of his learning too. This is a slow process and focuses on how he relates to others at lunchtime. Alex has started to seek out other children, and the mealtime assistant encourages him once he makes the first con-tact. She also explained how they give him prior knowledge of any changes, such as her assistant being away for the day on a course. She did mention that there was the question of how much prior knowledge to give him because he might, if he knows several days in advance, worry unnecessarily.

The kinds of teaching adaptations they used were explained by his assistant. He used to have a lined book for handwriting and leave spaces between the lines because his writing was very large. But now he writes in an ordinary exercise book, and although it is legible, there are still concerns about it. His memory for facts was described as good, so he did not need reminders of key facts. She saw her role as ensuring that he is focused. However, when he is to write stories, she will usually write the plans with him and then he will write from that. Alex was not the only child who could not write as quickly as they think. Alex joins a group for handwriting teaching twice a week. In addition, he does a physical exercise programme (Fun Fit) with another boy, which focuses on motor skills and hand-eye coordination.

Teachers, teaching assistants and other professional support

Alex's mother expressed some concerns that the occupational and physiotherapists had discharged him about a year ago. But the autism special teacher had visited the school to advise the teacher and assistant about his difficulties in understanding relationships. Alex has a particular interest in girls at the moment, and there was a concern about how he will manage at secondary school. He has shown an interest in older girls, has followed some around the school and shown an interest in being cuddled by them.

His mother felt that he was quite happy with his teacher and assistant, though he does not say much or complain. Alex particularly liked his last two teachers, who happened to be men. His mother said that his current teacher was keen to focus on getting Alex to do 'a little more work'. Alex said that he got on well with his teacher and talked about his teacher as 'working him hard'.

Alex's assistant described how Alex did not need to approach his class teacher much because she was there in class with him. She also talked about how she liaises and plans with the teacher. There are class teaching plans covering several weeks, which relate to the group in which Alex learns, and she uses these plans. So, she communicates briefly with the class teacher about what is needed before and after teaching sessions. They might even communicate by email if something is pressing. Alex's mother felt that his current teacher was more aware of Alex's needs than previous teachers. In the past she spoke with the teaching assistant: 'you didn't speak to the teacher'. This teacher had asked them about how he could best support Alex. Her response to this was ambivalent; on one hand she wondered why he did not tell her what he had been doing with Alex but, on the other, this was the first time a teacher had enquired in this way.

Alex's mother talked about how Alex was starting to be aware of 'who's going to help me' at secondary school which he goes to in just over a year. His mother saw his assistant as essential to his coping in class: 'he would probably lose interest quite quickly because she supports him to keep him focused and to keep him aware of what's going on at the moment'. She believed that, without this support, 'he wouldn't have made as much progress as he has'. Alex's mother knew that his assistant was experienced in supporting children with autism, but less aware of what her qualifications were for her support work. Alex's assistant had in fact done some training course for autism.

When asked how he got on with his assistant, Alex said 'good', while his assistant talked about having a 'really good relationship' with him. Having matured over the years he can even say 'something that's even a little bit cheeky'. But, he can expect his assistant 'to do everything' for him. For her there has to be a limit, and though she will support him, 'I don't need to do everything for him.' So sometimes 'he'll ask me to get something and I'll say "No – you can get that."' She realised how much Alex depended on her in class because, as she explained, if she was called away from him for a while, he would not start writing without her present. Or, if she was away, he would jump out of his seat and say he was finished, not knowing what to do. She interpreted this as her acting as a 'security blanket' for him.

What helps/hinders learning

Alex's mother had clear ideas about the kinds of approaches that help his learning. For instance, if there are several instructions, he needs them to be repeated or presented in a way that he can access. When writing he needs small reminders and prompts of what he is expected to be writing about. She thought that he can write about interesting matters and usually there is a flying theme in the writing. Alex's mother also emphasized the importance of preparing Alex in advance for any changes to his activities or routines. She noted that, although they often do this for Alex at school, sometimes they have not. As she explained: 'Well, there you are then, no wonder he wasn't happy, what did you expect?'

Alex's assistant believed that his being in the class rather than withdrawn was positive as he could see others doing their learning, feel part of the class, and that he 'should be trying to do the same as the other children'. However, noise can hinder his learning, such as others walking past the class; but these little things can mount up and make a difference.

Placement

Where at school

Alex went to the nursery school associated with his primary school. At first he spent some time in the nursery and some time in the assessment centre (discussed above). From the infants he then went to the junior section. Being a large urban primary school, the two sections were separate, and his mother did not initially realize how separate they were. She also recalled how they did not know at first whether he could manage at the local primary school or not. But, they tried it because they thought it would help him socially. They did however go to visit a special school, as well as another school that had an autism unit. Her concerns with the special school were its distance from where they lived and that the children from the unit, when she observed them in an ordinary class, sat in the corner of the class facing the wall. She found this separation in the ordinary class quite 'negative'. However, she liked the idea of a unit, and saw advantage in some withdrawal. But her position was that she did not want Alex to be somewhere where he struggled and was unhappy. She felt that he had been fine at this school, despite his 'moments' and 'blips'. Alex's assistant also described his placement as 'absolutely fine'. She believed that had he been in a special setting this would have affected his 'behaviour in a negative way'.

Other activities

Alex also takes part in wider school activities. He enjoys activities with the school chickens and rabbits and, as his mother mentioned, he has brought home some eggs. He has also taken part in some singing around Christmas time. Both his mother and assistant discussed how his mealtime assistant was able to get him involved in activities.

During the holiday periods, for two days a week and monthly on Saturdays, Alex has gone to an activity centre run through children's services. Holiday periods had been difficult for him, but he has come to like going because they do activities with children of different ages. For his mother, this has made 'such a difference', and 'he's enjoyed the holidays'. Alex's parents have had a care plan for him through a direct payment system which gave them access to care breaks, and this is how he went to the activity centre. But this was now being reviewed, and is going to be reduced. In the past, there was some flexibility; and, in addition to the centre activity, he had swimming lessons and they could pay for some days out, but this might now be reduced to just the activity centre.

Inclusion/exclusion

Alex's mother believed that there was a place for special schools, even if 'it's not relevant to him'. For her it was more about the support provided than the school: 'So if mainstream schools provided enough support to support everybody, then you wouldn't need special schools. But they don't; they don't have the wherewithal to provide the support.' Alex's assistant also believed that 'there's definitely a place for special schools'. She considered that some children would struggle in ordinary schools, adding that 'we're very lucky in that Alex is a very tolerant little boy . . . he has his difficulties, but with help he can overcome them and be seen to be very similar to his peers'.

Parental involvement

With teachers and other professionals

Alex's mother felt that she only knew a 'small amount' of what went on in school with Alex. She said that she would like to talk to them more often, though she and her husband saw Alex's teacher at parents evening and his assistant was also there with the teacher. She did recognize that his teacher was around and available after school. However, she saw his assistant every day when they talk about what has been going on during the day. She found this 'beneficial' as it meant she could then talk to Alex about it at home. This was especially important as Alex rarely told them about what went on at school. Alex's assistant also talked in a similar way about the afternoon contact she had with his mother.

Alex's mother used to have contact with other professionals, like the physio and occupational therapists, when he was younger; but no longer. They used to put programmes into the school. More recently, the school has decided that he may need occupational therapy for some of his care needs, such as dressing.

Disagreements and support groups

Both Alex's mother and assistant said that there had been no disagreements about meeting Alex's needs. His assistant did mention that his parents were a little concerned about the transfer from a Statement to the EHC Plan, still to take place.

Alex's mother had been part of a support group for the parents of children with SEN who went to a few local primary schools. She had enjoyed meeting up with other people and talking about their children. This was about sharing experiences, which she found 'quite reassuring'. Others would ask her about Alex 'to reassure themselves that their child isn't completely out of the ordinary'.

Social interaction

As discussed above, Alex's lack of interest in others was based on him being 'quite happy just being at school and being at home', as his mother put it. If he has shown interest it has been in older children, but as his mother said, 'he still isn't motivated enough to actually want to go to see somebody after school'. When Alex was asked in his interview about being with other children, he said: 'I like to be by myself', and that it was 'not often' that other children approached him. However, his assistant noticed that he became upset if he did not go to assembly with the other children, when he had his intervention group. She believed that he had a sense of belonging to the class. In addition, his mother discussed how other children were 'good at supporting' him at school. Some children even ran around after him to get things that he asks for, to the extent that 'he can almost get people to wait on him'. She had also heard from the assistant that when Alex is in a group in class, others invite him to join them.

Alex did not like games and sports, and so did not fit in well with other boys, as his mother described. She wondered whether not fitting in either with other boys or girls might become an issue for him when he is older. Overall, he prefers 'the company of girls', possibly because 'they they look after him'. Alex was also described as thinking that 'anybody who talks to him is a friend'. As his mother explained, he did not 'really understand the difference between knowing somebody and knowing somebody really well'. Though Alex has no siblings, he has several boy cousins who are older than him. Alex used to withdraw from them when they met. This was because they were active, energetic and noisy, but Alex has talked about seeing them.

Future

Immediate future

For Alex's mother, secondary transfer in just over one year is 'our next huge challenge. It's a difficult one to know what's for the best.' She believed that they will stay with mainstream provision for him, which was the conclusion from his annual review of provision. This is based on the progress he has made, and that he likes seeing children at school. She also talked about Alex liking to see other children from his school who go to the secondary school, so 'there's that part of being familiar with people in your community'. They have visited four schools and talked to the SEN coordinators to see what they have to offer. They are interested in whether there is a unit or somewhere the students can go, and also about lunchtime support. They have a particular school in mind, which is the local one where most children from his primary go.

When Alex talked about going to another school, he talked about going to a 'high school and then university'. He knew that a high school was for older children and referred to the specific school his parents were considering. His assistant saw his last year in primary school as the 'big year' for him before he transfers to secondary school. In her view, it was a matter of getting the right level of support for him. French was one of his strengths, and there was a risk that this might be dropped as a subject and the time used to catch up in other core subjects. Her worry was that he might get lost in a secondary school system, but was confident that his parents would not 'let that happen'.

Worries and hopes

Alex's mother was worried about him being isolated, teased or bullied at secondary school: 'you just don't know, because of him having different ideas and thinking differently'. She wondered who will look out for him as he was 'quite vulnerable'. Her worries were about his safety and his lack of self-awareness; he is 'quite often just in his own little world and getting on with whatever he needs to do', and she realized that his isolation was 'not something that concerns him'.

Alex's mother described how he wants to be an engineer and design aeroplanes or flying birds. He is aware of university because his father works there. She tells Alex that he needs to work on his maths if he really does want to do engineering. She seemed pleased that he thinks about what he would like to do in future.

10
Nina

Mother: 'Parent power is massive and not to ever forget that. The authorities are far more afraid to take on a parent than ever . . . never just accept something if you don't feel that it's right for your child. And I think that the main thing is to go and visit these places – every school or every college – with your child, and see how they react with your child while you're there.'

'There is definitely a need for special education placements in special schools, whether they be a special school or even a base in a mainstream school.'

Teacher: 'Get to know the young person . . . be person-centred. It's not about what you want; it's about what the young person needs. Give them process time; don't demand; speak to them in the way that you'd like to be spoken to. It's a really simple rule. But, you'd be surprised how many people don't do that. It's fun; it's not a battle to be won. You know. Try different things. Try different things. But definitely build a relationship.'

Background information

Nina is 18 years old and attends a residential specialist college for 16- to 25-year-old students with learning difficulties. She goes home every four to five weeks where she lives with her mother and her partner. She has an older brother aged 28. Nina is coming to the end of the second of her 3-year programme. She and her teacher were interviewed at the college, while her mother was interviewed outside the college.

Identification

Description

Nina described herself as 'helpful and loving to laugh', and as loving to be with people 'who love me', saying that there were 'loads' who loved her. Others found her 'funny', and thought that 'she was great'. She also mentioned that she liked countries, such as Luxembourg, and was quick to ask me if I had visited that country. She then explained that her interest in Luxembourg came from 'Lucy Lamp Light' from the Letterland books. In addition, she talked about horse riding, swimming, and playing with her friends. She also talked about liking animals, birds and plants.

Nina's teacher described how Nina had 'taken on' the character of 'Lucy Lamp Light', from a set of educational books about the alphabet. Nina carries four or five books around with her. Nina identifies with Lucy, who is portrayed as a kind and loving person who sends out light from a lighthouse to help people.

Nina's mother described how Nina was born with a very rare chromosome abnormality associated with a dislocated hip. Nina was also born prematurely and, as a 'tiny' baby, had tests to establish why she was small. This is when the chromosomal abnormality was identified and when her mother was alerted to the possibility of some type of learning disability. Her mother described how she felt: 'quite lucky in that I was prepared from the age of one'. Nina has very small hands and swan-necked fingers which makes fine motor skills very difficult for her. She has also had a mild scoliosis (an abnormal twisting and sideways curvature of the spine).

Nina struggled at pre-school with socializing, was diagnosed as having autism at 5 years old, and started primary school with a Statement. At that age she was able to read, which she learned from flash cards, and knew her colours and numbers. Her mother described how 'she was always getting herself into trouble' through her 'inability to understand other children's feelings'. However, she did make some friends, and 'a lot of children wanted to be friendly with her' because 'when she's obsessed about something she learns it to an encyclopaedic level'. Nina's knowledge of languages was described as 'incredible'. Nina has been learning German for two years and 'speaks German very well'. She was now learning French; her mother described her interest in 'countries, languages and capitals' as 'her current obsession'.

Nina's mother described Nina's educational attainments and abilities as above average when assessed at primary school. She was able to learn her times tables 'by heart', but she struggled with more ambiguous areas. Her mother recognized that Nina had 'learning difficulties' because 'she didn't achieve'. She felt that Nina might have achieved a maths GCSE because 'she's quite strong in maths', but Nina was not entered for this exam. She achieved one GCSE pass in art.

Nina's college teacher described her as 'highly intelligent', referring to her 'smattering' and love of languages and countries as well as her interest in the outdoors and nature. Nina knew the Latin names for plants and animals, but her teacher believed that, though Nina was 'really very clever', her intelligence did not match 'her abilities to undertake tasks and to carry things through'. Nina's concentration was variable, which her teacher linked to the autism. Nina was described as having special educational needs associated with her difficulties in transferring her knowledge to the written word; her 'writing is quite immature, although she's very good at spelling'.

Nina's mother also talked about how Nina has become more independent in everyday life. She can buy things from shops using cash as well as a debit card. As her mother explained, 'I've taught her that she must pay by her card because

I am reducing her risk factor there.' Her mother also mentioned that, when Nina started at the college, some of the teachers said that they were 'fascinated' by her, and as her mother explained: 'I've had this before. and I'm not just saying this because I'm her mum.' But her mother also described how Nina, over the years, has 'grown into some of her autism traits'. For example, when excited she will run about and hum. She also tends to ask other probing questions very quickly without realizing that this is not what people do. However, as Nina has got older there is less 'negativeness' from her.

When I met Nina she engaged me in a discussion about 'Lucy Lamp Lady' and the associated Fisher-Price toys. She explained that the toys were made in Belgium, which was near the Netherlands, but sometimes were made in Mexico or the USA. When asked how she knew this, she said that the details were from websites or on the bottom of the toys themselves. But, Nina was reluctant to talk about things being difficult for her. She said that she was 'OK'. But when asked if others might find things difficult about her, she did recognize that they would like her to talk less about Letterland and Fisher-Price toys.

Nina's teacher described Nina as 'absolutely fantastic' and that college staff had to 'learn to work with her'. Nina presented very challenging behaviours because her reactions were 'physical and verbal'; people found her threatening as a 'petite girl' who gets into 'such a rage'. She described how she soon identified that Nina's behaviours were linked to her fear. So, 'Now we've managed for 18 months to really work very well with her, and she's developed positive relationships, she really has begun to blossom.'

Nina's teacher also discussed Nina's response to stress, such as arm-flapping, how she can be in 'her own world a lot of the time', and her lack of awareness of safety. Nina could become stressed on others' birthdays and become contrary. So, when it was someone's birthday, she would tease the person by saying 'it's nobody's birthday today', till it reached a point when others would tell her to shut up. Nina can recognize when she might have hurt someone, according to her teacher, but she will often avoid talking about it. However, sometimes she will just go up to someone and say 'sorry'.

Impact of her difficulties, labels and others' reactions

Nina's teacher and mother both talked about how Nina would tell others that she has autism. Her mother described a recent episode when Nina met two young people with severe physical disabilities with their carers who came from a special school. She stopped them to say hello. Nina said to the carers, 'I've got autism, and I think it's important that everybody is nice to everybody even if they're different.' Nina's mother expressed how proud she felt by what happened, believing that Nina being open and accepting about having autism 'really helps'. But, her mother also explained that Nina's knowing that she is different has mixed implications for her. On the one hand, Nina was 'happy to be autistic when she reads that some famous people have got autism', but she can also be 'sad because she knows that she doesn't have as many friends'.

Nina's mother discussed how Nina's father could not accept Nina's difficulties and that their marriage did not survive. Her father had two children from a previous marriage who were 'very bright' and went to mainstream schools. He now had hardly any contact with Nina.

Nina's mother explained how her difficulties were put in the 'autism box, mainly for funding reasons', as there was not any 'identifiable name for it'. She also contrasted autism with Down Syndrome, which she saw as more visible and so more 'understandable' by others. Nina's teacher talked about Nina's mother searching for a reason for Nina's behaviour. But she felt that, despite labels being useful to some people who feel comfortable with them, labels cannot always be found, and they are not 'relevant to building a relationship'.

Nina's mother described some distressing experiences that they have had over the years concerning others' reactions to Nina. When Nina was at pre-school, some of the parents organized a meeting and decided that they wanted Nina 'expelled because they didn't want a special needs child in the school'. Even though the head teacher disagreed with these parents, her mother moved Nina as this was not the 'right environment'. From her mother's perspective it was hard when Nina was younger; Nina was 'a blonde little girl, who looked like an angel, and then suddenly would behave like the devil'. She described how 'people looked at you as if you were a very bad parent and had done something very badly wrong'. But, as she grew older, 'it became more apparent that she had special needs'.

Statement/Plan

Nina was issued with a Statement before she went to primary school. Her mother appreciated that getting a Statement early enabled her to appeal if she was not satisfied with the provision. The Statement had also been transformed into an EHC Plan, but from her perspective this had not changed the content. However, they get a direct payment which is now organized through adult services, since Nina is 18 years old. Nina gets a debit card, which enables a certain amount of money to be withdrawn. From her mother's perspective the card system works well, but Nina could not run the new system herself.

Nina's mother believed that without the Statement/EHC Plan system you cannot be assured about provision. Her experience of the annual review of special provision was of all involved meeting to go through how Nina was progressing in relation to the provision available. Though the content of the Statement did not change much over the years, she believed that there had been improved systems of monitoring Nina's progress at her previous special school and the current college. This included more specific measuring tools.

Learning: what and how

Provision

Nina's mother was very satisfied with the provision Nina received at the special school before she came to college. Nina followed a programme broadly in line with the National Curriculum which she felt was suitable for a school. Her only concerns were with Nina going to the library during breaks and sitting alone reading a book, instead of having social contacts through activities with other young people.

Nina's teacher described Nina's current college programme as a City & Guilds vocational course on animal care and horticultural conservation. This covered practical activities with animals in two placements. Literacy and numeracy (telling the time, weighing food, etc.) are embedded in these practical activities, and there is minimal paperwork involved. When Nina talked about her activities she referred to feeding animals and doing art – for example, making a lampshade on which she put Lucy Lamplight's name. She also talked about learning languages, not just at the college but at her previous special school.

Nina's teacher described her role in the college as coordinating the behaviour management plans. This involved collecting various kinds of information about students from before entry and integrating that with what they learn once students start. Nina's teacher also explained that they have an extended curriculum where numeracy and literacy are embedded in life skills at a suitable level for the student. This happens when students are on placements and outside formal programmes, such as when they are doing the shopping or sorting out laundry.

Nina's teacher explained that there is a very strong emphasis on social interaction in the college, and in this context there had been notable improvements in Nina's behaviour and relationships. She believed that all students needed to be valued and respected, with this incorporated in their personal support plans.

Importance of learning and engagement

Nina's teacher believed that the college being residential was a very suitable environment for Nina, as 'it's a first experience of being away from home'. She was very confident that the college was 'helping her with her social skills and her transferable skill base'. Nina's teacher also commented on how Nina was doing something 'she loves' on her programmes. Nina's mother described Nina as 'never happier than when she's learning'. But she did not like watching films; only liking documentaries, and reading factual books about birds, other countries and history.

Care assistants

Nina's teacher recognized that the care support provided by staff needed to be of a high quality; the students needed 'somebody with enthusiasm to lead ... but quite often unfortunately in the care-providing industry people do it for money – an attitude of "All I've got to do is sit and watch telly all day."' Her teacher recognised that the college sometimes used agency staff when they were very short staffed. She believed that some people worked better with Nina than others, and that other care assistants, who want an 'authoritarian control of things', felt less comfortable with Nina.

Nina's mother held similar views about support staff. She saw some as 'wanting to do a good job', but that a 'lot of them are brought in and trained on the job'. She believed that people like that could put Nina back in her progress if they 'know nothing about the unpredictability of her autism and her flashpoints'. Nina had her favourite assistants, both on the programme learning and the residential care support side.

What helps/hinders learning

Nina's mother believed that you had to stop Nina going into a downward spiral once she started, or it would be hard to stop it. She felt that what started this spiral was often 'someone working with her who doesn't understand the way she responds best', or tries to 'force her to do something'. Here, her mother talked about a primary schoolteacher who worked with Nina who used the image of a bridge to understand how to work with Nina: 'to make progress she's on one side of the river and you're on the other; you need to cross the bridge to her first and then bring her back to your side'. Her mother explained that this meant that 'you can't call her over; you have to join in whatever she's obsessing about at the time'. The idea was to start with being her friend and then 'pull her away from it', 'talk about it later and she'll go along with you'.

Nina's mother thought that Nina needed a small group of students and lessons that were not too long. Nina liked activities that were fun, but also 'loved things that are timetabled'. The key, according to her mother, was to 'use her obsession', such as when doing numeracy say 'well let's do it in Euros today'. She felt that 'sometimes people lack the imagination to do that'. What hindered Nina's learning was a noisy environment or learning from someone who was 'very strict' and who she could not 'warm to'.

Nina's teacher drew on her own background in counselling to suggest that what helped Nina was 'to recognize what her behaviours were about, what she was saying' and on the basis of having a good relationship with her addressing her concerns. Her teacher's role was to pass on the information and understanding about Nina to those working very closely with her. She also reinforced strategies in the plan they had developed 'to make sure that people followed it'.

Nina's teacher talked about how she reacted to Nina having a 'wobbly'. She talked to her asking if she had heard something upsetting – for example, Nina once heard about a pupil stabbing a teacher, something she heard on the radio. Her teacher would then offer to hold Nina's hand, which she might or might want to do. Or, the teacher might pursue asking about what upsets her as the key aim was to 'reassure her' and give her 'recognition that 'it's sad and it's scary but it happened a long way away from here'. In the case of Nina hearing about the stabbing, Nina 'started to be contrary and she started to shout and be very rigid in her movements'; so her teacher said to her, 'what would Lucy [Lamp Light] do and what would Lucy say?' And Nina said, 'Lucy would say "Oh dear"', and Nina 'changed her voice'. In describing what helped Nina, her teacher emphasized that Nina feeling safe at an emotional level was not just her responsibility but that of the whole team of those who worked with Nina.

For Nina's teacher, what made Nina less comfortable was last-minute changes, such as staff changes, and not giving her clear information about something. Nina also needed 'process time'; 'anyone who hurries her will have problems'. What interfered with Nina's learning were 'old school' control views which 'come from stuff in their own lives'. When Nina was asked about what helped her learn she answered in terms of what she liked learning. When asked again, all she said was that teachers helped her.

Placement

Where at school

Nina did 'very well' at her primary school, according to her mother, a school which was located in a small town. There were some 'ups and downs through primary school', but Nina's mother felt that the 'school was very supportive' and the head teacher 'fantastic'. This was partly about the school providing a 'care base for autism', a small classroom for about six children. Nina and the other children spent some time in the base and were also integrated in mainstream lessons.

Things became more complicated at secondary transfer once it was decided to go for a special school. The nearest suitable special school was in a neighbouring authority and Nina did not have access to this school. The local authority special school that she had access to was an hour each way in a taxi. Nina eventually went to this more distant special school. Nina herself talked about being at this special school as 'fantastic for me', a school where she had 'many different friends'. From her mother's perspective, the 'general ethos of the school and everything they offered was quite good' and Nina was described as 'very happy there', though there were 'our ups and downs' and often Nina was very tired from the travelling.

Placement decisions

Nina's mother explained that this special school was chosen because it was associated with more moderate learning difficulties (it was formally designated for children with 'varied complex needs and abilities, including moderate or severe learning difficulties, social emotional and behavioural difficulties and autism'). It was seen as more suitable than another special school in the authority which was for children with severe and profound learning difficulties, because Nina was 'quite able and it was felt that she could follow the National Curriculum, possibly taking one or two GCSEs'. So, though the school was suitable in terms of provision, its distance, and only having students to the age of 16, were disadvantages.

Transfer from the special school at 16 to college was also an issue for Nina because most special schools provide for students up to 19 years old, and so specialist colleges take students at 19 years old. The first choice of college was an agricultural-type of programme which was Nina's 'passion', but the college did not finally accept Nina because she was too young. Nina's teacher mentioned that she thought that Nina's mother wanted a residential setting because Nina 'needed something to bring her out of that autism, to support these behaviours that were blocking her relationships'.

Nina's mother felt that the college rejection had a 'very negative impact'. Nina's mother also explained that had she known that the other local authority special school (for severe/profound learning difficulty) was to be reclassified to accept less severe learning difficulties, she could have moved Nina to this school which taught students up to 19 years old.

Two city further education colleges had been considered, but seen as unsuitable for Nina. Nina's mother wanted a residential setting, and these colleges were too large, with thousands of students. The local authority initially wanted Nina to go to this kind of college, but Nina's mother explained that Nina experienced problems at one of them while at the special school. So, when Nina and her mother visited one of the colleges she told the staff that the visit was to satisfy the authority. The staff were 'quite happy to say that Nina's not really suitable for the college'.

Initially the local authority did not want to fund a residential specialist college placement. But Nina's mother argued that when the travel costs to the city college are taken into account, a residential special college might not be more expensive. She also showed them the letter from the college about Nina when she went a day a week from the special school. So the authority agreed to the current specialist college placement. Some of the reasons for choosing this college were that they wanted a residential setting, and her mother did not want to live too far away from Nina. But, one of the issues now was that Nina was the youngest in her year group in the college and she will be leaving when she is 19, while the others leave when they are 21 years old.

Inclusion/exclusion

Nina's mother had very clear views that separate educational settings were 'absolutely' needed. She believed that primary schools were 'fine' and they 'worked', but at secondary school 'children are very cruel and differences open up with mainstream students'. In addition, 'any child with a special need is much more vulnerable to bullying and being ostracized'. She quoted what Nina had told her – what she called 'a very profound saying': 'when she's with mainstream students generally she feels like the ugly duckling and when she's with special needs children she feels like a beautiful swan'. Her mother mentioned that this is what she told the psychiatrist who was 'quite taken aback that that's how she feels'. For Nina's mother, Nina 'likes being with other people with special needs; she understands that they are also different'. Nina's mother's views were explained in terms of her beliefs that 'we all flock together don't we, we socialize with people that are similar to ourselves . . . we're comfortable around people that are the same as us'.

Nina's teacher held some similar views to Nina's mother. She had attended a comprehensive school that was 'inclusive', but in her experience it was 'absolutely brutal for some of the pupils with special needs'. Her view was that, although 'it is fantastic to think that our community can embrace and celebrate difference, it is a load of cobblers quite frankly'. Her position was that 'specialist colleges like this can work intensively with students to reduce that level of support, so you're working towards independence'. For her, what they were doing was 'life-giving' 'it (inclusion) is all about saving money'.

Parental involvement

Nina's teacher felt that relations with Nina's mother were 'excellent' and that the relationships were 'respectful and honest'. She saw Nina's mother as very focused on the 'very best for Nina'. There might be episodes when they disagree over something, but from her perspective 'it's never a problem'. From Nina's mother's perspective, relationships with college staff were 'very good'. She realized that they may feel, 'oh my God it's her again', when she makes contact. Her attitude was that 'it's not a popularity contest . . . I'm there to make sure that my daughter gets the right support'. As she said: 'I'm not averse to telling them when I think they're failing.'

She also talked about her relationships with various professionals involved in Nina's health. Overall she felt that they had been very fortunate with the paediatrician, their GP and psychiatrist. The GP had, for example, shown an interest in Nina living away from home at college, and the paediatrician had taken a wider interest in Nina's hobbies. However, when Nina turned 18 she had to change her psychiatric care and this was irritating to Nina's mother as there was not a named psychiatrist any more, just a team where the psychiatrist might not know about Nina. Accessing mental health services was not always easy, taking several months to get an appointment. Nina's mother felt that once a child had a Statement/Plan there ought to be immediate access to this kind of service: 'by the time something goes wrong you don't have nine weeks to wait'.

Disagreements

Nina's mother had some issues and disagreements over aspects of Nina's provision over the years. For example, she had concerns about Nina's taxi ride to the special school and the very early hour that she was picked up. Despite complaints to the authority and the local MP, she described the situation as 'that's the way it is'. There were also a few issues over the residential side of Nina's college provision. She was concerned about the 'low wages and massive turnover of staff (support workers)'. These workers did not know the students, something which worried her 'massively'.

Nina's mother also had some concerns about what Nina did over the weekends. She described herself as being 'on the warpath' about this matter, as she was unhappy about Nina sitting in her room and not becoming involved in various activities. She talked about how she confronted the new college principal about whether students rode bicycles on a footpath, as was shown in college website publicity. But she did emphasize that she 'always tries to keep it friendly and not fall out with them, but equally, if I don't stand up for Nina there's no one else in this world that will'. However, when it came to resourcing and placements in relation to the Statement of SEN, Nina's mother felt that the authority had been quite responsive. She had never had to go to Tribunal to get what she felt was needed. She knew people who had gone to Tribunal but she felt that she was 'very organized in my paperwork', and this helped. She felt that 'they know if somebody's going to put up a good argument and be difficult to get past. They're very crafty, they know parents that are going to roll over.'

Nina's teacher 'admired' Nina's mother 'very much' and recognized that Nina's mother was a 'formidable woman' who was 'fighting for Nina to provide'. This teacher recognized that 'people with learning disabilities can often be treated as second-class citizens by the medical services . . . there's an element of "let's not bother", which is really quite shocking'.

Support groups

Though Nina's mother was not currently a member of any parent support groups, she was currently working with a local care group that had plans to provide supported living through a social housing company, a group that wanted her to join the board of directors. She explained that she had not previously got involved in such groups because she had 'concentrated all my efforts on my problems with Nina'. However, she had had some contacts with a rare chromosomal group and the National Autistic Society.

Social interactions

Nina's mother described how other children would at first see Nina as different: 'she's a bit odd'. But when they start to talk to her and she tells them about an 'Asian ladybird which has got ten spots', they start to think differently, especially when they hear that 'she can speak three or four languages'. But, in Nina's mother's view, it takes time to get to know her and 'that's the stumbling block'. Her mother also talked about a girl she met at primary school who is her 'best friend', someone who was 'incredible' with Nina and who Nina was very comfortable with. As her mother explained, 'sadly not every young adult is like that'.

Nina's mother described Nina as typically getting on better with the teachers at school and college than her peers. When talking with Nina, she felt that she got on well with the teachers and care workers at college. She was reluctant to say very much, other than she also felt she got on well with the other students. This contrasted with what her teacher described about her college peer relationships; other students did not like it when Nina became stressed and it was then that she tended to be contrary. However, her teacher also described Nina as 'really funny; she's very smart, she gets the subtleties of humour'.

Nina's teacher said that she did not consider Nina as popular among the student peer group; she 'did not really have any positive relationships with students', something she related to 'a lot of our students being autistic'. However, there were two male students who 'look out' for Nina, who seem to understand her and even sometimes speak up for her. This peer support reflected what she described as the college's focus on peers 'looking after each other'. Nina's mother thought that Nina was quite interesting to others, but that Nina was not bothered. Her mother also explained that this was her attitude to her boyfriend with whom she went to the College Prom.

Nina's mother described how her family struggled with Nina 'a little bit'. While Nina's grandparents tried very hard with Nina, her brother and his fiancée were described as 'amazing' with her. The other members of the family do 'struggle', but 'would never say anything'. Nina's mother described how people in their neighbourhood would invite Nina round when other young people were invited with the adults for a social gathering. But she would decline the invitation for Nina because, if she came with her, Nina would not know what to do, and this would affect her mother spending time with others. This was a question of her mother also having her 'own needs' and how children of her mother's friends' responded to Nina; they 'wouldn't be seen dead with Nina'. But there were some who had time for Nina, such as the daughter of the man who used to taxi Nina to school for five years. Nina's mother thought that this came through her father's influence; 'he was a special guy who thought much of Nina'.

Nina has shown little interest in her father, according to her mother, and has recently refused to see him. Her mother felt that Nina 'could do without anybody else' besides her. Nina tells her mother that she loves her and cuddles her, telling 'people at college that she misses her mum'.

Future

Immediate future

Nina's mother found it 'very difficult to look that far ahead'. Though sometimes Nina surprises her mother in what she can do, her mother sees her as still very young. She has a year to go at college and then leaves at 19. Her mother is considering supported living, but does not think that 'she'll go into a work placement very quickly', because 'she's too immature'. She wondered whether when Nina is in her mid-twenties a work placement might be possible. Her mother had considered another college placement, like the one that turned her down before, but worried that the authority might not fund another three years. It was clear that Nina's mother saw that she would have to 'fight' to get a residential setting for Nina. During her interview Nina talked about supported living and the upcoming placement visit.

Nina's teacher believed that Nina was fortunate to have a mother who will 'make sure that she's in the best possible place'. Her teacher talked about how it is hard for the parents of the young people at the college, as they had expected their children to become independent. Nina could be expected, she felt, to have 'an enriched life', but that others 'are always going to have to help her'.

Fears and hopes

Nina's mother's main fear was about 'when I'm dead and gone'. She was very grateful for Nina's half-brother who will be trustee of a trust fund set up for Nina. She would like to see Nina with a partner/boyfriend, but she fears that Nina will be 'lonely'. She recognizes the difference between her, for whom loneliness is 'the worst thing', and Nina, who is 'not a sociable person and being lonely for her is not something she feels'. Her mother expressed that this was 'hard for me to accept'.

Nina's teacher feared that Nina might be around people who 'don't get her', to which she could 'shut down'. Her teacher's hope was that Nina's mother continued fighting for Nina. She hoped that Nina will be happy and have an enriched life, saying that, 'she's got so much to give to society, her knowledge and her humour'.

Future plans

Nina's mother's plan was 'to get her as independent from me as possible before I die'. This would involve supported living near to where she lives, so they can 'meet once or twice a week, help her with her shopping, she can still come for Sunday lunch but not come back and live with us'.

Nina's teacher felt that Nina did not have any sense of her future and rarely talked about it. However, she had talked about having a baby, but her teacher thought that Nina did not know what this meant. However, in interview Nina did say that she would like to 'save people', and be a lifeguard. She also talked about being an 'artist' and then said an oil worker for Letterland.

11

George

George: 'Ask them what they need and like, what they sort of want, and don't sort of just force things upon them that you think might help . . . there's nothing more annoying than being patronized or being forced into using something that you don't really think is necessary.'

Mother: 'Encourage as much as you can because they are capable of doing more than you think. It's a frustration that they say that they can't do it, but if you persevere, it can be done.'

Advisory teacher: 'Do not make assumptions about anything, but also do not impose limitations . . . to have in your head "the sky is the limit". There's no impediment to helping the child to have a go at anything and everything . . . take notice of what he says – he's the lead.'

Overview

George, who is 15 years old, goes to a large urban secondary school. He lives with his parents and his younger sister, age 13, who went to the same school. He was interviewed, as was his mother, with his father present, at home. The advisory teacher for visual impairment, who had supported him from childhood, was also interviewed.

Identification of needs

Visual impairments

George's parents noticed his eyesight problems when he was about 12-weeks-old. His mother talked to the health visitor who referred George to the hospital when he was about 9-months-old. He has been diagnosed with nystagmus, and over time with other conditions such as optic atrophy, divergent squint, and cone dystrophy. He has had two squint surgical operations because the first one did not work.

As the advisory teacher explained, the nystagmus involved involuntary movement of his eyes, resulting in reduced vision. His mother also referred to his other diagnoses also involving a loss of vision, and that there was little that could be done about the optic nerve damage. George described himself as short-sighted and not having very much depth perception. He was aware of the diagnoses, explaining that he sees slightly better in darker conditions rather than when it is bright. He showed how he is able to read something when the page is about 10 centimetres from his face, and said that he cannot see people when about 10 metres away. He could also explain how print needed to be enlarged and on gold paper to give more contrast for reading.

His mother elaborated in more detail about his visual abilities. She explained how he finds looking at a busy picture difficult – when standing up he cannot see some things on the floor, nor see the white/blackboard in class very clearly. It was only more recently that his vision seemed to stabilize; he now only has annual appointments with the optician and no longer goes to the hospital for check-ups.

The advisory teacher described George as having a severe visual impairment, noting that he does not look like he has an eyesight problem. But, when people get to know him they notice it from how close he sits to the TV, reads a menu or book, and likes enlarged print.

It was notable that, when asked to describe himself initially in the interview, George did not focus on his impairments and additional needs, but on his personality and abilities, by contrast to his mother and the advisory teacher. He felt he was outgoing to some extent, had a dry sense of humour and was quite determined. Though he admitted to not usually thinking about himself in these terms, he said that he was quite good at mathematics, computers and electronics. He recognized that he was 'not good at ball sports'. He thought that he could do his school work, but that his 'handwriting was terrible'. He admitted that he would put a lot of effort into doing the activities only if he has some interest in them. He was less sure about what his parents thought about him, but thought that his mother sometimes thought that he 'did not have a clue'. George's view linked to the advisory teacher's account of how his mother had talked to him a few years ago about the need for him to 'pull his finger out' and put in the effort he needed in order to get on in life.

Changes

The advisory teacher explained that George was very anxious at the early stages of primary school because he found quite a lot of things very difficult. Learning basic skills was very difficult for him. When he visited George there were occasions when George was in tears because learning was so hard for him. He believed that this was compounded in the early days by the visual impairment and his teachers not understanding the severity of the impairment. The advisory teacher included himself in not understanding how difficult things were for George then. He did not believe at first that the nystagmus would interfere that much with his learning and development. But, as he became more involved in George's primary education and the additional diagnoses appeared (optic atrophy and cone dystrophy) and their significance for his learning became evident.

The advisory teacher suggested that at that stage George would have been described as having learning difficulties. However, as George's progress accelerated this view of his difficulties changed. George had 'a very spiky profile' at that time, but when the advisory teacher discussed things with George, he noted his very wide vocabulary, making him believe that 'there was a lot more going on than he was able to demonstrate with the basic skills'. It was important from the advisory teacher's perspective to see functioning in a learning context; his functioning 'depended on things other than his nystagmus, such as how he felt about all sorts of things'.

Implications of the diagnoses

George's mother described how she felt 'devastated' when she first had the diagnoses at 9 months and was told the 'worst scenarios of what he wouldn't be able to do'. She also described some of the implications she has noticed. When he passes somebody on the street on the opposite side of the road, or even close by, he would not spot them. She explained how when he was at primary school he struggled because a lot of the learning was from pictures on the wall and around him; he missed out on some of these experiences. She also envisages more problems arising. Though he has had a bus pass for years, he will not use it because he is afraid of getting on the wrong bus. She also described how George sometimes becomes very frustrated with his visual difficulties, becoming 'stroppy'.

The advisory teacher thought that George was more sensitive about his impairment when he was younger, when 7 to 9 years old, than now. But, even when he visits him in school George prefers to have meetings outside rather than inside the class to discuss the adaptations made for his learning. This was to avoid others asking about the visitor observing him. He emphasized the importance of the school, understanding that George wants to have more control over the support he has, something that would be expected from any teenager: 'I think he's become more of an initiator of change that suits him.' The advisory teacher attributed this partly to George's key teachers having understood the importance of George having some control and being independent. The advisory teacher believed that this growing independence was 'something to do with himself, but partly with the kind of support he's had'. He also talked about George going at about 10 years old to an outdoor activity centre for families of children with visual impairments. George was determined to walk along a very high wire secured by a hoist about 30 feet above the ground and not be beaten by this challenge: 'to have a go at things, even if he was frightened'. With his swimming and sailing, the advisory teacher also saw a strengthening of George's self-belief.

The advisory teacher suggested that George might see his opportunities and success in swimming and sailing as a positive arising from his visual impairment through the organizations for people with disabilities. George himself agreed with this view saying that: 'I think it can be positive, 'cause you get to do things that you wouldn't have got to do otherwise – the sailing I do, I do at a much higher level than I think I would do if I was normal – there's a lot less people in the field, so you can move further in it.'

George was able to express that he was 'OK' with his visual impairment, having got used to it: 'So I don't really think I wish I had perfect sight; I get on with it.' However, he agreed with the advisory teacher that things were more difficult for him when he was younger. He would think then: 'Oh why have I got it and not someone else?' He explained this in terms of struggling to play with balls when younger, but as he got older he moved to activities that did not require seeing small things. He also described how his mother tended to avoid asking him to look for anything because he was unlikely to find it, which suited him. He commented that his mother worried about his road safety and being bullied at school, while his father was more concerned about the driving to take him sailing in other parts of the country. He felt that she worried about him 'probably more than she should'.

George's mother described how there was more disappointment about his condition when he was younger and his vision was unstable. She recognized how, with 'all the help and assistance he does get at the school', he was getting on so well now. However, George recognized that his visual impairment had affected his mother more than his father. The advisory teacher's views were consistent with his mother taking the lead in advocating for George. He also noted that she had become more relaxed since the more anxious primary years. He attributed this to the change in George who was 'academically doing very well, and socially and in terms of his leisure pursuits . . . he's doing so well, that I feel it's less of an issue'.

Labels and disclosure

As the advisory teacher explained, George was registered as sight-impaired and his parents were satisfied with this category because they saw it as opening doors and leading to better provision for George. From his perspective he felt cautious about labels as some parents, in his experience, liked to gather labels; for him, the 'important thing is the individual and what's appropriate for their needs'. This agreed with what George's mother said about the 'severe visual impairment label'. She explained that the label was appropriate, 'because they do have special needs, so that label is absolutely fine . . . they do need specialist paper and some equipment and, you know, so that term is absolutely fine. I don't think that's derogatory'. George explained that he talked about having a visual impairment and did not talk about having nystagmus. He also said that the term 'disabled' did apply to him in the visual area, but not others. The term 'special educational needs' meant to him 'all the help I get at school', and he felt that he did have special educational needs.

The advisory teacher described how George, like other young people, did not like to be marked out as different by being observed by him in class. George had also been concerned about being marked out by the teaching assistant support he received in class. But George was 'much more accepting of that now because he feels that he can be in control of it'. This was because he was now able to say when he needed support. His mother noted that George had a monocular, but he did not like using it because it made him stand out in public. She felt that this might change as he gets older. From his perspective, George realized that others would notice his visual impairment when they started to work with him, but at school those around him know about him and they barely notice and, if needs be, would help him out. However, he did say that he usually tries to make his visual impairment not so obvious – for example, when getting glasses he gets 'something that blends in'. Neither his mother nor the advisory teacher thought that George currently experienced any bullying or discrimination. From George's perspective, there were some nasty comments when he started secondary school, but no more after those incidents.

Statement of SEN

The advisory teacher explained that getting a Statement of SEN on the basis of nystagmus was hard when George was younger. But, as George's additional needs became more apparent, the case for a Statement grew. His mother said that she had been asking for a Statement since pre-school, but she was told that George did not need additional support. From her perspective, it was not 'until he'd had the same teacher (in year 2) that he'd had in his foundation class, did she realize that he wasn't a naughty child'. This teacher came to see that George was frustrated because he could not see. So, she was the one who then pushed for the assessment to be done. For his mother the Statement meant that 'they didn't then treat him like he was a naughty child'. She also felt that he would not have got where he was with his learning without a Statement: 'he would have come out of primary school, I'm sure, without being able to even read or write properly'. She saw no disadvantages to having a Statement, except that she wanted to be involved in choosing who worked with George in class. This was because 'the first teaching assistant had been completely wrong for him'. In his interview, George remembered that 'the teaching assistant I had wasn't very good'. The advisory teacher, in this regard, commented that George's mother expressed strong parental views and always 'made sure that the Statement contained all of the aspects'. Though the local authority was converting Statements into the new Education, Health and Care Plans (EHC) Plans, this had not happened for George yet. For his mother she did not see any changes to his provision arising from this conversion.

Learning: what and how

Educational provision

From the advisory teacher's perspective there were no issues with George's primary provision. Though there was unlikely to be full continuity of provision as teachers and other staff were different, there was 'a very positive attitude to provision, a very positive attitude to any recommendations I made, and I think that they bent over backwards to try and get things right for him'. From his mother's perspective a key part of George's primary provision was the advisory teacher's termly visits and advice and the one-to-one support from the teaching assistant. Various resources were made available for George, such as gold-coloured balls for physical education lessons.

Secondary school provision was described as 'pretty good' by the advisory teacher in terms of the adaptations made and staff sensitivity. He has visited most subject lessons over the years, though he recognized that provision is less good on occasions when supply teachers are involved. From his mother's perspective, provision was very satisfactory, because George 'comes home quite happy'. At secondary school the teaching assistants are in the class maybe at the back or sat near somebody else. If he needs their assistance, he indicates in some way. She also felt that she had enough information about George's learning and progress, commending the SEN coordinator as 'brilliant'. George's science and maths teachers had the skills to adapt their teaching to his needs. He had never said that he could not do an experiment in class. His secondary school had also painted all the steps yellow for him, which was refreshed each year, and doors which he used had larger letters': 'so they really adapted the environment for him . . . that's very good'.

George was positive about the support he received, saying that 'when I didn't have the support, everything was a lot harder. And now I've got it, this actually makes my life a lot easier in school.' But, he did also recognize a negative side to this support when assistants stay next to him when it is not needed. He also explained that a 'teaching assistant can be quite restricting . . . when they did not know what's sort of wrong with me'. The advisory teacher considered that all of the National Curriculum has been appropriate for George. He is unlike other children he supports who have additional orientation and mobility needs. However, he qualified this by saying that, though George gets round his current environment well, this may be more difficult for him in the future in new environments – for example, when going to college. Overall, the advisory teacher described the kinds of adaptations George required: almost always sitting at the front of the class to optimize what he sees on the board, lighting that was not too bright or glaring, enlarged print on a high-contrast background. Sometimes a teaching assistant would produce a copy of what was on the board and, on occasions, he might have a printed copy of what's being discussed. However, on other occasions George 'might manage with print that I would think would be too small for him, probably again for social reasons: "I don't want to make a fuss about it."'

Provision reviews

The annual Statement review process was based on information from all his teachers about George's attitude, attainments and the assistants who worked with him. His mother felt that this one-hour meeting was better than parents evening meetings. George, who was present at the meetings, was described by her as 'hating it and squirming' at what he hears. This has been mostly very positive: 'It's never been derogatory. They've always said that he's really good, his attitude is excellent, he learns well, he's a pleasure to have in the class – maybe just a little less talking sometimes.' The advisory teacher also explained how, on the basis of these reviews, the SEN coordinator produces a summary sheet with action recommendations that would go to all staff members to use in the lesson planning. He has, however, had his doubts about to what extent these recommendations have been used when such a large number of people are involved. In his view it comes down to the particular assistants who work with the pupil. Though he believed that the assistants who worked with George had 'always been very good at implementing those things', he has had cases where he had 'to remind them about the discrimination Act and reasonable adjustments'.

His educational needs

From George's perspective he had recently chosen his GCSE option subjects, and this represented what was relevant to him – computing, electronics, maths and science. He admitted that he did not think much about what he needed to learn more widely for his future. It was in this area that his mother felt he needed to learn more life skills in addition to his GCSE subjects.

All were agreed that what George needed in educational terms was common to all other young people of his age. His mother saw George's educational needs as only slightly different from those of others: 'It's really only the enlargement.' She explained: 'It is just the eyes. So as long as he's got everything enlarged that he needs to, and he's given the extra time that he needs to process it when he's writing anything down or doing a test or anything, and he sits at the front, which is where he prefers to be, he's absolutely fine.' From George's perspective there was a small minority who learned like him by listening, while most watched videos and wrote things down. But, he did believe that he needed a less 'chaotic' type of teaching, by which he meant more organized teaching that did not try 'to teach a lot of things in quite a short period of time'.

Teachers and teaching

His mother felt she can call the SEN coordinator and discuss any issue. George was also not afraid to go and see her and mention issues to his teachers. He likes most of his assistants as well, except for one who did not get the hints he gave her about his support. His mother noted that George was well liked by his peers and adults at school. She also suggested that he did not 'mess around because he doesn't get the clues from the other kids . . . so he never gets himself into trouble 'cause he can't see what's going on around him'. George was clear about getting on well with his teachers, who provide everything he needs. There were, however, a few who 'don't really accept my visual impairment as much as other teachers do'. He gave, as an example, a year 8 PE teacher who gave him 'wildly unsuitable' activities, compared to a year 9 PE teacher who, when others were doing table tennis, suggested he go off to the fitness suite gym.

The advisory teacher believed that George's teachers did not have enough preparation to adapt their teaching. Though teachers and assistants can come on a specific course about visual impairment, he believed that the cost prevented this happening enough. In his view, the teachers at George's school relied on the information from him and the SEN coordinator. His mother's perspective was focused more on the difference between the primary and secondary school SEN coordinators. In her experience, the primary SEN coordinator taught a class part-time, so had less time than the secondary coordinator. She also felt that she had less knowledge than the secondary coordinator about visual impairment.

What helps/hinders learning

George, his mother and the advisory teacher, expressed compatible views about what helped or hindered his learning. The main focus was on the use of enlarged yellow-paged books which his school made available once it was recognized as crucial for his learning. The advisory teacher also mentioned that teachers need to understand that someone like George might use lip-reading and so not stand with their backs to the windows. Given his nystagmus, teachers also needed to not move around the class a lot as this requires George to change his focus. By contrast, his mother talked more about teaching that captured George's interests in the sciences, for example. She also noted that George liked 'strict teachers' and 'controlled classes'. This agreed with what George saw as 'chaotic classes' which did not suit him. For George, making extended notes negatively affected his learning, because he saw this as just writing and 'taking it in', not understanding the content. He also talked about how the PowerPoint slides were enlarged for him, and how a teacher would ask him regularly if he could see and things were OK. Overall, he felt that he had enough say in how he learns.

School placement

There was agreement that ordinary school was the best place for George to attend. The advisory teacher had advised his parents before primary–secondary transfer that this was his view, though he did have some concerns about very large secondary schools. He felt that George would do better in a smaller secondary school from a pastoral care perspective. His mother said that she and her husband accepted the advice they received and felt George was getting on very well there. For George, his secondary school was 'quite good, and better than going to some other school'. He was clear that he 'preferred going to a mainstream school than going to one for just people with special needs'.

As regards more general beliefs about separate/special schools, the advisory teacher explained that the circumstances in which George would be better placed in a special school these days would be if he had extremely complex needs, which he did not have. He felt that the 'general trend was that the majority of parents want them to be in mainstream schools . . . they are going into mainstream schools and being well supported'. George's mother's view was that 'special schools are more appropriate where a child has a visual impairment and other difficulties as well'. She described how the special school for visual impairment 'used to be just for visual impairments; it's not any more . . . it's for some very severe cases'.

George had gone there with her to a group for three months when he was a toddler, but she stopped going because he began to copy some of the children's behaviour.

George's reasons for preferring a 'mainstream school' were about having more opportunities and receiving a 'better education'. As for any disadvantages in being at an ordinary school like his school, he thought that anything that did not work initially could be sorted out after about a year. For him 'inclusion' meant 'not segregating anyone, letting everyone in, giving everyone equal opportunities'. Inclusion 'stops anyone with a disability being pushed to the side, and it brings a lot more opportunity'. However, he did recognize that 'sometimes you can go a little too far with trying to include people . . . by not giving enough help or just trying to make people feel like overly normal and sort of ignoring the things that they need'. George felt 'as included as I want to be . . . I don't want to be like over-normalized, 'cause I think like without the help that I get I would be doing a lot worse in school'. It is relevant to his views about inclusion that George was a member of a sailing group for people with visual impairments, as well as a member of his local sailing club. He liked taking part in both.

Parental involvement

George's mother was very satisfied with the consistency of support they had had from the advisory teacher who has supported George for many years. She contrasted this with the advisory teacher support that other parents of children with visual impairments had experienced. He was described as knowing George very well, trusting him, and taking a wider interest in him than his schooling; he would have a chat with George 'like you might have with a mate'. From the advisory teacher's perspective his relationship with George's mother was fairly good: 'She's known that if she asks about things I will try to do something about them.' However, he did note that, on a few occasions, he found that what she felt about an event was not similar to what George had felt about the matter. In the context of the primary school about George's learning, he also thought that the primary school might have seen her as quite demanding. George's mother explained how she had asked several times for the teaching assistant to be changed at primary school, but the school refused, saying that the assistant had a contract till George left in year 6. Her view was that, as parents, they should have been consulted about the assistant and that 'maybe it would be good to have two because you get a break from one person'. She explained how George came home some nights very annoyed with the assistant. However, the matter was never resolved, and they agreed to disagree on the matter. But, the advisory teacher noted that there had been no serious disagreements over statutory assessment and the Statement of SEN. He said that others would have known about her concerns, and things would have been sorted out.

George's social interactions

George's mother has also been a member for several years of a local parent network related to visual impairment. Through this group, George participates in various activities – for instance, his sister had gone with him to a social event at a local restaurant with other young people. The family had also participated in outdoor activity centres. George also swam three nights a week. But, his mother still felt that he was 'socially outcast' because he does not go out: 'I see his friends out in town all the time, but he doesn't.' She explained that if he goes anywhere he likes to go with one of the family: 'He doesn't really like going anywhere on his own.' She wanted him to make arrangements himself with people, and when she and her husband raised the issue, he 'clams up and get stroppy'. The advisory teacher also noted that George was quite guarded about talking to him about becoming more socially independent. His mother also described how his sister wound him up by calling him a 'loner'.

The advisory teacher described George as popular and having friends, unlike some of the other young people he supported. He felt that 'his self-esteem is not going to be the same as other young people's'. However, both his mother and the advisory teacher talked about George being the focus of a national BBC programme about visual impairment. He was comfortable with this TV programme and his mother felt that it helped him. George felt that his teachers liked him and he felt a sense of belonging to his school. He also expressed that it was good to have friends 'who actually sort of care a bit, and also people who are willing to understand what's wrong with me'. He was able to talk about a specific friend who he had known for quite a while, 'he's like really inclusive and we're really good friends . . . we've both taken quite similar options' (he does not have an impairment). He said that they saw each other outside school; they had been paintballing a few weeks ago and they go out on his boat. George's view was that he kept away from others interested in sports and that, as regards friends, he was 'happy with what I've got really'.

His future

George's mother saw George doing A levels either at his current school or at a nearby further education college and then going to university to study something in the computing/electronics area. George saw his future in similar terms. The advisory teacher agreed with this, saying that George is expected to achieve good GCSE pass levels. He also saw no reason why, with adaptations, he could not succeed at university and find a professional type of job. With his sailing and swimming George can expect to live a full and successful life: 'if I'd looked at him and thought that far ahead when he was 7, I wouldn't necessarily have thought that was possible'.

His mother explained how she reminds him that 'because he has got his visual impairment he has got to have as best an education as possible' to get a decent job. But George had some of his own ideas. He wondered about becoming a video game designer and if he could make some money he could retire and buy a yacht: 'that's where I want to end up really'. He also wondered about running a sailing club. But, he did realize that on account of his visual difficulties travelling might be hard for him. He explained that when at a station or airport he could not see the information on the boards, so he would have to find someone to travel with him.

The advisory teacher had no serious worries about George's future, 'unless things happen that exacerbate his feelings about his visual impairment'. His mother felt that George had 'the gift of the gab so I'm sure he'll find somebody to put up with him . . . I'm sure he'll be fine'. For George, one worry was about being unable to drive and he considered that there might be a few limitations in what job he did, but this did not seem to discourage him. As the advisory teacher said, what George has is his 'cognitive ability, drive and determination'.

12

Julia

Mother: 'Good communication is key. If as a parent or teacher you have a query, ask, and ask early. Keep talking, little and often. For us, having one key link person who I have regular contact with made all the difference.'

Key worker (teaching assistant): 'As a parent you know your young person best. If you have any concerns, keep communicating until you feel things are resolved.'

Background information

Julia is 13 years old and attends a secondary school in a small town. She lives with her parents and a younger sister, aged 9 years, in a rural area near the town. She was interviewed at school, as was her teaching assistant, her key worker. Her mother was interviewed at their home.

Identification

Strengths and difficulties

Julia's mother described how they did not know that Julia had any disability till she was about 6 to 7 years old, when she was diagnosed as having Friederich's Ataxia (an inherited disease that causes progressive damage to the nervous system). At age 7, Julia was running around and there were no obvious problems; while now she cannot stand and is 'completely reliant on her wheelchair'. Her condition has progressed quite quickly, 'quicker than we expected', as her mother explained. 'However hard she works she's still getting worse' was what her mother said. Julia's assistant confirmed that Julia was quiet, but described how she was able to move around the school, managing to fit in, and that other pupils know her and her needs.

Her mother described Julia as very much like a teenager: 'she can be moody and stroppy as girls her age can, but she can be lovely and she's got a good sense of humour . . . she laughs a lot and she likes the dog as well'. Julia was also described as reading a lot and being 'quite shy', which her mother suspected was 'partly her personality anyway, but . . . it is exacerbated by her difficulties'. Her mother considered that Julia was 'very able', but 'very lazy academically'. She felt that Julia could do much better, attributing this partly to her personality, but also 'partly things are more difficult for her, and the other thing with her condition is that she does get very tired'. Julia's teaching assistant described her as 'very articulate, very bright'.

During her interview Julia described herself as 'really shy', but then explained that she was not really that shy with people she knew. Julia's 'big love of her life' is horses, but she also likes computers. From her mother's perspective the good thing about liking horses is that it gets her out, especially as it is too easy for a child with physical difficulties 'to be reliant on computers'. Julia gets more screen time than her sister, something which her mother felt was justified because Julia has physical difficulties. Her mother, despite not liking horses herself, realised that, for Julia, it was 'great that she's got this, and she loves going to the stables'. But she had to stop riding about two months ago because it was hurting her back. Julia is developing scoliosis for which she will have surgery, but there is a long waiting list.

Julia's tiredness is related to what her mother called the 'physical stuff she has to do' arising from her condition. Fatigue is also a key symptom of her condition. She described how Julia can transfer herself at school for the toilet, but she struggles with it. As her condition progresses she is becoming more reliant on help for things which she finds very difficult. At home Julia does not mind her mother helping her, but her mother wondered about how she will feel as she gets older. At school Julia 'doesn't like people helping with things like toileting', as she used to do it on her own. She is now helped by her teaching assistant.

Julia's mother described how Julia finds it very hard to write: 'she can write, but it's very, very hard work for her and she couldn't write a piece of work at school'. In maths she can write an equation, but 'it's so much work for her to write it that she's losing time'. From her mother's perspective, 'the tiredness is her biggest difficulty'. She had recently spoken with Julia's assistant about whether Julia needed extra learning time on account of her tiredness. For Julia, her favourite school subject was English; she liked 'doing stories and creative writing'. She talked about liking to read most kinds of books. Writing was done best by using a keyboard, but she felt that she did not write 'very quickly', which was about 'half a page in ten minutes'. She also described how she had just completed a piece of work which her teacher said was at an 'A*' by GCSE standards. However, she said that she did not like maths: 'I just don't like numbers; they just don't really make sense to me'; but said that she liked learning science. Her teaching assistant said that Julia complained about maths 'the same as everybody else moans about doing maths', but she was 'very good at it'.

Diagnosis and impact

Julia's mother described how they came to realize that Julia had physical difficulties. Her partner initially thought that Julia had mild cerebral palsy when she was at primary school, while at the time one of Julia's teachers had concerns about her physical abilities. So Julia went to see her GP, but it took about a year before she was seen by more specialist doctors and they got the diagnosis, about 7 years ago, when Julia was about 7 years old. Julia's mother also explained that the ataxia affects her fine and gross motor functioning as well as her speech: 'everything's been affected'. In addition, she could also be at risk of having heart problems.

Julia's condition was described as having 'a huge impact on her socially', noting that she is very isolated. This was partly associated with some very low level of hearing loss, but her hearing was also affected by her being lower down in a wheelchair. Her mother described how, when Julia is in town with some friends, 'they're all up here and she's down there and she can't hear them'. The effect is 'she doesn't want to go out because she's not really being included'. In her mother's view, 'I don't think people mean to exclude her, it just very easily happens.' Overall, her mother felt that 'it has a huge impact' on Julia; having 'periods where she does get very upset about it and very sad'.

Julia's assistant, who knew the family before Julia started at secondary school, described how Julia had become increasingly aware of her condition. Julia had 'started to ask questions of her mother – Why and what's happening?' Her assistant also described how Julia has 'times of depression', but probably did not recognize her feelings as such. For example, there had been days when Julia had been very sad and her mother would contact her to explain Julia's feelings, so they could be aware of them at school. Julia's assistant also discussed how Julia was 'getting used to certain ideas as she's going along, because obviously its progressive'. For her assistant too, Julia's tiredness was the 'biggest thing' that affected her. Her assistant also discussed how Julia did not like talking about her condition generally, and that she did 'see herself as different'. But, if Julia has to or needs to talk about it, 'she will talk about it with me', as her assistant explained. This reluctance to talk about her condition was also shown when I interviewed her.

Julia's condition has had 'a huge impact on all of us', was how her mother described the impact on the family: 'everything takes longer and is more difficult'. The family tries to 'get on with life as normal' as much as possible, but 'it is difficult'. For example, they do not go to the beach, because it is difficult for Julia and she 'hates going'; as she has 'got bigger it's got more and more difficult to physically manage'. Julia's assistant described the impact on her family as 'massive', referring also to how they have to come 'to terms with everything that's changing in their daughter and what the future holds'.

Labels and others' reactions

For Julia's mother Julia had no additional needs, as she was 'very bright; very able', but Julia was seen as having special educational needs as she found physical activities like writing very hard. Julia understood that special educational needs were about 'needing extra help to learn', and she recognized that she needed 'more help than other people my age' in writing. She talked about sometimes needing a scribe and using a laptop. However, Julia did not think she was 'disabled', a word she was reluctant to talk about. This reluctance was confirmed by her assistant, who explained that Julia sometimes said that everyone was disabled.

Julia's mother talked about how Julia 'hated people staring at her, and people do stare'. This means that she often does not like to go to 'new places' where people might stare at her. This was something that her mother talked about struggling with: 'She's very intellectually able, but because she's shy she doesn't like to speak up. So, when people see a child in a wheelchair, they'll ask her something, she'll look at me and it's trying to get her to answer.' Julia then gets upset because she feels that 'people think she's stupid because she's in a wheelchair'.

Overall, her mother described how people at her school 'have been really good', and there has only been one incident when she was in year 7. One of the boys told her, 'You're stupid because you're in a wheelchair', which was very upsetting for her. But one of her friends stood up for her and told the staff about the incident. Her mother felt that times had changed and there was not 'any overt bullying now', but that there was something much more subtle going on: 'people just don't include her and they don't speak to her and they don't involve her'. For her mother this effect was made worse by Julia's shyness. As her mother described, 'people stare at her, but then they almost don't see her at the same time'.

During her interview Julia talked about the year 7 incident as well as how people who do not know her draw the wrong conclusions about her. She understood that this was about her being quiet and shy, that being in a wheelchair meant to some others that she could not do things. Her teaching assistant explained that the school had a zero tolerance for bullying, and that she had not noticed any teasing or bullying towards Julia.

Statement/Plan

Julia was issued with a Statement when she was at primary school. The head teacher told her mother that it was good to start the process early as it took very long. From her mother's perspective 'it's definitely been useful because she got full-time assistance'. However, she felt that 'it has always felt very cumbersome; you get sent piles and piles of forms. And you know my partner and I are both sort of reasonably intelligent people, but sometimes you're wading through it. You wonder what are they on about.' She also said that she did 'not quite know how you get all the right information from all the right people and make it simpler'.

Julia's mother discussed how her experience of Statements was that they had to emphasize the worst case scenarios about how Julia was on her worst days to get the appropriate support. If they put down what she was like on good days, they would 'get less support'. So when they read the Statement, it did not look like her: 'it's just so depressing'. But she did realize that, with Julia, 'because she's a well-behaved child – she's very bright academically – it's about physical stuff'. She saw that 'physical difficulties are much less contentious than emotional or behavioural or learning disabilities'. Julia had not yet had her Statement converted into an EHC Plan; that was coming next year.

Part of what was important for her mother was the annual review of provision for someone like Julia where things 'always change a little bit'. But, she added that when she attended the annual review, she already knew what was going on. The assistant, who she considered was 'fantastic', kept her informed about what was going on and had been done through regular meetings. Julia's assistant talked about how these regular meetings enabled her mother and herself to address 'any issue that crops up'. Her assistant also described how Julia would come to the reviews and would say if she was unhappy with something. The others involved would include the community nurse and the therapy professionals.

Julia's assistant talked about Julia's care plan, which is part of her Statement. For her, Statements involved a 'very difficult' process because 'it's a very heavily paper-weighted . . . and involves ticking boxes'. But, she recognized that 'in ticking those boxes it means that they get the absolute care they need'; so, for her, 'it's the right thing to be doing'.

Learning: what and how

Provision

Julia's mother described the head teacher at the primary school as 'really support-ive' and as someone who 'fought to keep' Julia there by making adaptations and finding a way. But, her mother also recognized that the head might not 'have been like that if she (Julia) hadn't been a bright academic well-behaved girl'. In this way Julia's mother realized that 'the system has been less contentious and worked better for us'.

Her mother was very satisfied with the provision at Julia's secondary school too. Where she has issues with the school, it was 'to do with the school as a school, not to do with her difficulties'. This was the school where Julia wanted to go because it was the local school, and the school had experience of supporting other children who used wheelchairs. When Julia started at the secondary school she had full-time teacher assistance and, not long after that, said 'I don't want them following me around at lunchtime and at break.' The school responded pos-itively to this request, despite her mother thinking that they might have a 'battle about this'. The school has also been responsive to Julia's request to not always have a teaching assistant in all her lessons. So, in some she has no assistant, in others they 'hover in the background' and in others 'she has one and uses them quite a lot'. Julia's mother also talked about how Julia could come out of classes to take a rest if she was feeling tired. But her mother did not at first know that this was an option.

There was an issue for Julia's mother about Julia not having enough home-work. Her mother wondered if, because Julia was well-behaved, some teachers did not talk to her about homework, because they 'don't want to put pressure on her'. Her mother also felt that some teachers did not always understand Julia's needs. For example, there was a school trip in year 7 and it was not accessible for Julia, so she did not approach the school. But, when mentioning this to Julia's assistant, she was told that if Julia wanted to go, there was an area support service with an accessible minibus. But, it turned out that Julia did not want to go.

Julia's assistant explained in some detail the subjects that Julia studied. In addition to the core subjects (English, maths and science), she will study business studies and photography next year as option subjects. She may stop one of these options to enable her to have some more rest time. In addition to Julia's care plan, there is an individual educational plan and a transition plan about her future learning. The educational plan is accessible to all her teachers, so they can look up and see what she needs to learn in lessons. Her assistant also discussed how Julia felt 'very uncomfortable' receiving some support that she needs. Julia wanted to be independent, so that she 'moves around the whole college site on her own with friends'. This has been agreed with her parents, but her assistant mentioned that there was a 'fine balance between her safety and her independence'. So, if she has to use the lift she needs to be accompanied by someone, and she also carries a radio on her chair so she can contact someone if there is an incident or emergency.

Julia's mother explained that others say that Julia needs more physiotherapy, but, from her perspective, Julia finds it so difficult to stand. Julia has a standing frame, but 'she hates it, and a lot of the time it's very uncomfortable'. There is always the issue of 'getting that line between it being painful and being uncomfortable; I don't think it's ever less than uncomfortable for her', was how her mother put it. Julia really likes swimming and she does hydrotherapy. Julia's assistant explained that the physiotherapist and occupational therapist (OT) have visited the school. Now that Julia goes to hydrotherapy Julia no longer sees the physiotherapist at school. The OT would be involved if the school needed advice and support over tasks such as toileting.

In her interview Julia was quite open to talking about the support she needed in her learning. She described how she needed someone to scribe for her during assessments and when there is a booklet which is too small for typing on. She was positive about her school because others were welcoming and made changes for children in wheelchairs. She also talked about dropping PE and art in year 7. She has used these times instead to take a rest: 'I get really tired, so I have periods where I just go inside and I have a rest and read and stuff.'

Capabilities, engagement, and what she learns

Julia's mother and assistant believed that Julia was capable of achieving very high grades at GCSE. They both were confident that she could achieve 5A*–C grades at GCSE, or even better. However, her mother was concerned that she did not have very much homework. Her mother was unsure if this was the same for other pupils, or whether Julia did not do her homework and plays on the teachers, conveying the attitude: 'How can you give detention to a child in a wheelchair?' Her mother mentioned that she did 'worry a little bit that she's not made to do as much work as some of the others'.

Julia's teaching assistant felt that Julia enjoyed school and was 'happy with what she is learning'. Julia did not mind going into lessons with everybody else.

She also described how Julia will communicate when she is in pain, though when she first started at the school this was more difficult for her. Sometimes she will tell her assistant and this will be passed on to her teacher, but this does not happen often.

Julia's mother and assistant and Julia herself all believed that she needed broadly the same kind of teaching as other pupils of her age. Her assistant did, however, identify some challenges that Julia experienced in subjects which required manual dexterity. How Julia copes with these activities is being monitored and, as mentioned above, she is withdrawn from art, so she can use periods to take a rest. However, as her assistant emphasized, she does the same as others so as to make her 'be included': 'we are very, very keen to make absolutely sure that she does do the same as everybody else, within reason'.

Adaptations

Julia's mother described how she scribes for Julia when doing her maths. She also talked about Julia's electric wheelchair which enables her to get round the classrooms. There is also a specially designed room for her to have a rest and lie down on a bed. During lessons there are her friends who help her by getting her a computer. Her assistant described an incident last year with the English teacher when Julia found it hard to manoeuvre her chair because of how the chairs and tables were organized. Julia told her assistant about this, who then had a word with the teacher who rearranged the layout to better suit Julia's access.

During lessons, when pupils need to collect materials, the teacher organizes the class so that the materials are on the table where she will work. Other pupils are sometimes asked if they will volunteer to work with Julia. According to her assistant, this works well: 'they do adapt things so that she doesn't have to go all around the room'. In this way she takes part in lessons, such as science. Julia's assistant also explained how there is now a hoist both at school and home. Julia did not want it fitted at home, even though there was one at school. They have also had to adapt the height of the toilet seat so that it was at the same level as her chair to enable easier transfer. It is these types of adaptations that are recorded in her care plan. Her assistant summarized that these adaptations for Julia were 'about making sure she can get to the lecture, get to the lessons, making sure she's comfortable and that she feels able to learn because she feels comfortable'.

Teachers and teaching assistants

Julia's mother felt that Julia's relationships with her teachers were 'probably a lot like most of the other kids; some she hates, some she loves'. Her mother did remark that, as a parent, she had little contact with most of the teachers. Julia said that she liked her teachers because they are 'really helpful'. Her mother identified two or three teachers who were really engaged and 'got on well with her'. But, sometimes Julia's mother had experiences which made her think that other teachers 'don't quite know what to do with her'. She gave as an example an English teacher who, at a parents' evening said that she did not have enough information about Julia. For

Julia's mother this was a strange comment as English was Julia's strongest subject; she was achieving A's and A*s. Julia's mother described how she asked the teacher what else she needed to know, to which the teacher replied that she did not know: 'I haven't been told anything.' This teacher was considering moving Julia from the top class, as it was a large class, to a lower-achieving group. Julia's parents were so worried by this that they spoke with Julia's assistant, who then raised the matter with the SEN coordinator and head of the English department. The teacher left the school, but the episode indicated to Julia's mother that, for this teacher, Julia was 'a complication too many'.

For her mother the teaching assistant, who is Julia's key worker, is 'just fantastic'. When she speaks with her she finds her assistant to be 'one step ahead' of her and she 'always completely gets it'. Julia's mother also felt that Julia really liked this assistant and 'trusts her'. So, Julia's mother mostly related to this assistant who coordinated the work of the other assistants. However, Julia's mother recognized that some of the other assistants supporting Julia in class might be less well qualified. She recalled a cookery class when the usual assistant was away and there was another assistant supporting her in class. Julia came home very excited about how much she had done in cookery by herself. For her mother this was about a different assistant enabling Julia to do more of the cooking herself. This showed her mother the importance of expectations for what Julia could do. This incident also linked to Julia telling her mother several times that she did not need a teaching assistant and asking her mother to 'phone the school and tell them I don't want a TA at all'.

Julia's assistant had been working at this school for nine years and been Julia's key worker since Julia started in year 7. She had a high-level teaching assistant qualification and had previously worked as a dental nurse and librarian, also having a university degree. She was now the lead assistant who coordinated the other assistants, seeing her role as aiming to 'build the independence for everybody so that they can achieve on a personal level'. She saw her role with respect to Julia as ensuring that 'teachers were aware of her condition within reason, aware of her educational needs and what she needs to do to learn'. She understood that teachers could not know everything about her condition, which was partly because there were confidentiality issues too.

What helps/hinders learning

Julia's mother believed that were no particular approaches that helped Julia in her learning. She referred to electronic equipment as relevant, such as her laptop and an iPad, which they were thinking of getting for science so Julia can photograph her experiments. Julia, from her perspective, also felt that there was no particular teaching approach that helped her. She believed that she received good-quality teaching at the school, and that the teachers understood her needs. Julia's assistant explained that the teaching assistant team tried to encourage Julia to take responsibility for her learning in class. This might involve encouraging her to ask the teacher, rather than the assistant, for assistance, if she needed some.

Placement

Current school

Julia's mother described how Julia changed primary school from one in the nearby town to another in the village near where they lived. Julia had not settled at the first school, so they tried this other one where the head teacher was committed to making it accessible for Julia. Julia's assistant believed that her current secondary school was very suitable for Julia, describing it as an 'inclusive placement'. They have pupils with a range of SEN/disabilities – for example, pupils with autism who do not communicate. In her experience, young people with severe disabilities might go to a special school, but not once they started at the school; the parents would have decided in advance of secondary transfer.

Placement decisions

Julia's mother discussed how she had not seriously considered a special school for Julia. She once did think about it when she heard about a special school aimed at children who are academically able and have physical disabilities like Julia. But this school was in another region of the country and they did not want her living away from home. Were there a similar school locally that she could attend daily, then they might have looked at it seriously. They had also been told that Julia could go to a grammar school and they should not assume, because of her physical disabilities, that she could not go. But her mother had ethical issues with such schools and it would mean at least an hour travel each way to the closest grammar school. In any case, Julia really wanted to go to her current school as her friends were going there. Julia confirmed this when she was interviewed. Julia's assistant believed that Julia gets on well at this school academically, and that a special placement would be 'wrong', socially and emotionally, because she 'needs to learn amongst her peers'.

Outside school activities

Julia has started to do an activity called horse agility, now that she cannot ride horses. As her mother explained, this is like dog agility and it enables her to do it while on the ground, not riding a horse. Julia has also gone to an activity centre for people with disabilities. Families go too, and this is where Julia's mother met another family with two children who use wheelchairs, with whom they have stayed friendly. Julia likes going but 'finds bits of it difficult'. For example, in the dining room there are other people, some with intellectual disabilities and autism; her mother thought that Julia 'finds all that quite frightening'. Her mother added that other people also did and that she herself found it intimidating too. On another occasion Julia was invited again, but was uncertain about going. Her mother took her there, but she did not want to stay. They had also been told about a youth club for children and young people with disabilities. Julia's response was 'Why would I want to go there?'

Julia talked about her own horse, which is near where they live, so they go to see the horse regularly. In addition, she talked about hydrotherapy, which she does with a physiotherapist. She described this as swimming.

Inclusion/exclusion

Julia's mother believed that there are children, not like Julia, who have complex learning or behaviour issues; for them, by 'putting them in mainstream schools you're just isolating them'. She wondered whether sending a child to an ordinary school might 'look like inclusion' but not be. Julia herself was not that clear what inclusion meant. But she did think that describing a school as inclusive meant that it was 'really welcoming'.

Julia's assistant believed that there are instances when special schools are suitable for some children and young people. She gave, as an example, pupils who have severe disabilities, such that they might 'go into special care' when they are older. She also discussed an example of a girl who was being considered for this secondary school. She had significant 'behaviour issues' as well as Down Syndrome, describing how this girl did not 'interact with her peers in the primary school. It was the behaviour difficulties that meant that 'she wouldn't get any social benefit out of here'. However, Julia's assistant did think that her views and approach had changed a little over the years. She said that she 'fights more now for more extreme cases . . . where it benefits the child'. She believed that this was because she saw that, with research, there were ways that had not been tried before: 'I think the further you go along, the more you find out that you can do these things.' She described herself as 'always up for learning more . . . and finding out more from people'.

Parental involvement

Both Julia's mother and her assistant described a very close working relationship with each other. The assistant described how Julia's mother would let her know if something 'goes wrong', using emails or phoning her. Relationships with other professionals were less straightforward for Julia's mother. For example, she discussed how the occupational therapist who was working with Julia at primary school at the time when Julia's condition was getting worse, said that the school could not be adapted for her, and that Julia needed to move schools. This was very upsetting for Julia's mother, because Julia was 'so settled there and so happy and I didn't want to move her'. Julia also had to see many different professionals and this 'takes an awful lot of time'. For example, in the last six months they had two weeks in which there were five appointments. With the cardiologists they have seen five different doctors, so that Julia and her mother do not know who they are talking to. Part of that problem was that the doctors and other professionals did not communicate between themselves very well; as her mother noted, 'I don't think they do very well and you know you go in and you tell the same thing.' This reached a point when she told them that 'this is not good'. So they have established that they can see the same person. As her mother explained, 'they were absolutely fine with that and I have found that if you ask you can get'.

Both Julia's mother and her assistant said that there had been no major disagreements about the content of Julia's Statement. Julia's mother also discussed how she has belonged to an international internet group for parents of children with Julia's condition. This has provided some very useful information. Other than that, she did not belong to any other support group.

Social interaction

Julia's mother described that things were difficult socially for Julia because she becomes tired at the weekends after a week at school. After school, on one day a week she has hydrotherapy and on another day she sees her horse, as she also does at weekends. It becomes a choice between seeing her horse or visiting a friend, and Julia will 'always go and see the horse'.

During her interview Julia talked about her friends at school and how they do things for her if she asks them to. Her assistant talked about Julia liking her own company; for example, 'sometimes she'll carry on sitting and reading while her friends are sitting there'. Julia did not, in her view, want more social interaction than she already had. However, Julia did laugh and joke with her two best friends at school. Her assistant also talked about Julia having some contact with other pupils at the school who used wheelchairs. Julia might greet them when they meet, but there was no sense of common identity.

Julia's mother described Julia's relationship with her younger sister at home as 'just like sisters': 'they squabble and they argue'. In her view, the younger sister did not 'always appreciate how difficult things are for Julia'. The younger sister has less time on the computer compared to Julia at the same age, while Julia's younger sister can do other activities more easily. Julia sometimes may resent her younger sister having a friend to visit, to which her younger sister tells Julia that she could invite someone around if she wanted to. But, as her mother commented, 'it's not that easy because she does get so tired'.

When Julia was at primary school, and was using her wheelchair, she was sometimes invited to her friends' homes, but according to her mother not as much as other children. When Julia was smaller their parents could carry her if their houses were not accessible. Now she is a teenager and bigger, she has had some invitations. On two occasions Julia's mother has stayed with Julia during the visit. Sometimes Julia wants to invite friends to her house, but because of her tiredness this does not happen often. Her mother also felt that Julia has 'some anxiety about whether they would come or not, and also when they came, what would they talk about'.

Future

Immediate future

Julia's mother discussed how Julia wanted to go after her GCSEs to a college where she could do equine studies. This is what Julia also talked about in her interview.

Her assistant discussed how her immediate future depended on whether her condition plateaus or not. She saw this as a possibility, drawing on her knowledge of the condition. Julia did not, however, like to discuss the future with her assistant, though her assistant knew that Julia's future would be about horses. Her assistant also commented about her parents; that 'they are amazing because they've had to learn as they've gone along, because as you can appreciate she started off as a little child who was walking and talking and everything was progressing'.

Worries and hopes

Julia talked about being scared about her GCSE exams. But when asked about her future after school, she said that she had no worries. By contrast, her mother worried about Julia going somewhere different when she left the current school and whether she will get the kind and quality of support she currently experiences. There was also a worry about changes in funding and whether adequate levels of funding will be available. When she spoke recently to the local authority in response to a circular letter about post-16 provision, she was told that 'they can't guarantee anything, because budgets change, so what they do and don't provide also changes'. So this was a worry about whether Julia 'won't be able to do what she wants to do'. But, it was also about the state of her condition and whether it plateaus or not.

One aspect of hope for Julia's mother was that researchers around the world were working on finding a cure. The research team had raised funds and she heard one of the specialist talk in London a few years ago about a possible cure in about five to seven years. Her mother felt that this development 'gives her (Julia) a lot of hope'. Her mother also explained that Julia is aware of the situation which they have spoken to her about, treating it 'like you do sex education. We've told her what's appropriate for her age and if she asks something we tell her'. They try to 'stay positive about there being some sort of treatment'. They also keep on about her doing more physiotherapy, even though 'she finds it so difficult'. While her parents 'desperately hope that this treatment will come', Julia envisages doing an equestrian course, and one day 'setting up my own horse-breeding stud'.

13

Tricia

Father: 'Keep communicating, don't give up, be as pushy as you possibly can. You have to go and learn about the disability as we're mostly fairly ignorant as a population, unless we are forced into it. We just sort of go with the flow and you have to be proactive.'

Teacher: 'Always be optimistic; always be optimistic but realistic. Don't set them up to fail. A lot of students do fail because there's so much pressure for them to pass. Work with them, get to know them, find out where their limits are as soon as you possibly can, and work to those; maybe push them a little bit, obviously, but you really need to have a flexible approach.'

Tricia: 'Sometimes my parents worry me a lot, because they want to help me a lot and they want to care about me. But I say, "I'm fine. I can do it. I want to do it." Sometimes I say "Help me, I'm a bit stuck" . . . sometimes things go wrong, sometimes they go right. . . but I like a little help.'

Background information

Tricia, who is 18 years old, attends a further education college part time, and a school for the deaf part time, where she also boards during weekdays. She lives at home in a rural area with her father and mother at weekends. She has a brother who is 24 years old. She and her teacher were interviewed at the school for the deaf, where she had a support worker to assist with communication during the interview. Her parents were interviewed at home.

Identification

Description

Tricia's teacher described her as 'bubbly, eager to please, generally a very happy girl, always got a smile on her face and always chirpy'. She described herself as 'a very happy person. I'm very cheerful at college and . . . very interested in learning.' Her teacher also described her as sensitive at times, when 'things might get on top of her'. Her father described her as having grown up to 'be a fairly intelligent, very emotionally charged, outgoing person'. He considered that she was 'quite a well-rounded individual'. Tricia's teacher expressed a similar view about her by describing her as functioning 'extremely well with both hearing and deaf people'. He described her as someone 'that's kind of on the fence' and that she has 'a very good speaking voice, which could be better with a bit more speech and language therapy'.

Her parents explained that she was born to a hearing family with no history of deafness and that she was diagnosed at 11 months, though they suspected this before then. Tricia is profoundly deaf, having a vestibular hearing loss. Her father described her unsupported hearing loss as 'quite profound' and that she uses a hearing aid in one ear and had a cochlea implant in her left ear five years ago. She uses a 'total communication' approach, which means an element of hearing, an element of lip-reading, assisted hearing and British Sign Language (BSL). Her father explained that Tricia also had a 'slight dyslexia' which 'in a deaf person compounds the problem to a larger than average degree in a hearing person'. Her teacher talked about her having 'processing problems', which he could not specifically trace back to the dyslexia recorded in her Statement. The processing problems were influenced, in his view, by her emotional state: 'If she's agitated or upset by something she becomes quite close-minded.' So, his approach was to say to her, 'Ok – I want you to get your hair back, glasses on.' He found that this signalled to her to be 'open-minded and receptive to information', and he found that 'it works'.

Tricia's teacher summarized her attainment in literacy and written work as 'behind in age-related terms', which he attributed to her deafness and other factors. She was struggling to reach a C grade in GCSE English. Tricia also talked about English being 'very difficult' for her. This was about reading and spelling some words, and she recognized that she needed help. Tricia's teacher taught her maths, where she was studying a functional mathematics programme, not GCSE. She was currently working on collecting and using data, and he found that she struggled to process and retain information.

Her teacher also described her as needing and receiving 'quite a lot of pastoral care' to support her emotionally. Her parents strove to do the best for her, from his perspective, to get her the best opportunities. In protecting her they may have set their aspirations a little too high. Tricia described her parents as being very proud of her when she 'keeps working and focusing'. Her interests were in 'supporting people', and she felt she was 'good at health and social care', which she was studying at college.

Impact of deafness

Tricia's mother felt that Tricia would see the impact as a negative one. Her father elaborated further by saying that, in his view, as she matures, 'she sees the disadvantages, but that when she was younger, certainly in her early teens and earlier, she didn't see it'. By this he meant that she had to work harder academically to achieve. Her mother gave as an example, if they were at a restaurant and Tricia wanted to go to the toilet, she would suggest Tricia goes to ask someone where it was. Tricia's response would be 'Oh I don't want to do that', so they would practise what she would say to ask for the toilet. But her parents recognized some positive aspects too. Her father talked about her communicating to her friends across a crowded room using sign language. Her father explained how she uses it to her advantage by switching off her aid when they have an argument.

Tricia's teacher found it difficult to comment on the impact of deafness on Tricia because this was a personal question for a deaf person. He also found it hard to answer because, in his view, Tricia 'coped so well in both worlds'. He explained that there are deaf people who wished they were hearing. Then there are others; he thought that Tricia was like this, who would say: 'Actually, I'm quite lucky; I can dip into both.' He saw Tricia as quite open-minded and different from what he called the 'other extreme' view, which was: 'I'm quite happy to be deaf. If I get married I want my children to be deaf.' He described her as 'comfortable in her own skin' and her being part of the deaf and hearing world as her parents had encouraged.

Her father found it hard to answer the question about the impact of Tricia's deafness on the family. He did feel that, compared to their older son, they worry more about her personal safety and realize that she will have to 'work harder at things to obtain the same academic qualifications as him'. Tricia's mother talked about going to evening classes to learn BSL, and mentioned that 'having a child born to you who is of a different culture is quite difficult'. Tricia's father said they would do what it takes to support her, such as moving to an urban area to support her when she finishes college and gets a job. He also explained that Tricia's older brother had wanted to 'distance himself from it for a long time', but since completing his degree 'will not hear things said against disability in general and deafness in particular'. Tricia's father also mentioned that their wider family had become more deaf-aware.

Labels and others' reactions

Both parents considered that Tricia had a special educational need, but doubted that Tricia would herself be happy to use this term about herself. Her mother felt that Tricia did not 'realize exactly how she is'. When she reminds Tricia to wear her hearing aid and use her cochlea implant, Tricia has said that she does not need to as she has a CSW (a communications support worker who interprets for her). What Tricia does not appreciate, according to her mother, is 'how reliant she is on the CSW at college'. Her father explained that, not just with deafness, but drawing on his experience of people with a range of disabilities, 'if you've never had it, you don't miss it . . . she (Tricia) doesn't regard herself as being special . . . we're almost the unusual people'. But he did believe that, as she has matured, she has understood that she has a disability because 'she doesn't have an asset that other people have'.

When Tricia was asked if she had a special educational need she talked about having a CSW, which seemed to be a yes, but then said she did not know. When asked about having a disability, she said 'Not much. I am only deaf. That is all.' Tricia then explained that she saw herself as having a disability and not having a disability, what she called 'both', and that 'I feel I'm quite in the middle.' But she did say that being in the middle was a 'little bit difficult'. By this she meant that understanding what some people say can be difficult: 'That's why I'm in the middle; but I prefer sign language.'

Tricia's mother wanted Tricia to make her deafness more visible, as she believed that if people know you have a disability they will be more helpful. As her mother explained, Tricia had long hair and she keeps it down to cover her hearing aids, so 'nobody else knows that she's deaf'. Tricia's father said that deafness was sometimes called a 'hidden disability' because when someone walked in the road you would not recognize it. But, he did realize that concealing deafness can be an issue for children and young people. By contrast, Tricia's teacher felt that Tricia was more comfortable with having a CSW with her at college than other students, who would want the CSW to sit far away from them in classes. Tricia was described by him as 'confident when in college', even when with her CSW and her cochlea implant were visible. Tricia herself seemed to take a view about the visibility of her deafness which was in between her parents' and teacher's. She talked about her partner as someone who did not want to wear a hearing aid, by contrast to other friends who did not mind wearing one. She herself sometimes wanted to conceal her aid and sometimes was willing to show it. She described herself as not like her partner and as someone who was 'very proud to have an aid'.

Tricia's mother talked about how Tricia had to work hard to retain some of her hearing friends from when she was younger. Her father described how Tricia had experienced a lack of insight from a group of her friends when younger. For instance, when with a group of friends, they talked about going outside, but she did not understand their talk and nobody explained their decision to her; so she was left behind. Her father saw this kind of incident as a 'misinterpretation' reflecting a 'lack of forethought on part of the hearing community', rather than discrimination. Tricia's teacher could recall only one incident of drunk young men who harangued her and a friend one evening, but that was a one-off event.

Statement/Plan

Tricia had a Statement, from about 13 months old, which her parents explained was arranged by the advisory teacher for the deaf. Their experience was that they had to 'fight' to get speech and language therapy to be written into the Statement. Tricia's father explained that if they had written it into the Statement, they would have had to 'go out and get someone and employ them in the area to do that'. For Tricia's father this issue was overcome by her going to a school for the deaf, where they have 'enough deaf pupils to warrant the employment of a speech and language therapist'. He recognised that 'it would be very difficult to do that' for one child in a primary or secondary school.

They had another issue at the time when Tricia was 12 years old and was moving from a local school to the school for the deaf, some distance from home. They recalled some tense meetings, and Tricia's father talked about being called a 'pushy' parent, but felt that he did not 'mind being labelled like that'. Part of the issue was to make the case that Tricia needed to be educated more than ten miles from her home in an urban area where the school for the deaf was located. Tricia's father saw the issues as 'coming down to money', but they had not needed to go as far as going to Tribunal to get what they felt Tricia needed. Despite these issues, Tricia's father felt, in hindsight, that the authority compared to others across the country was 'quite innovative and committed'.

Tricia's parents saw advantages to having a Statement. This was about having a written document that stated what was required and that the authority was accountable. Her father explained this view in these terms: 'It makes things accountable for people who are not deaf aware, who are only maybe interested in the financial side of things rather than anything else.' Tricia's teacher also believed that Statements give parents 'more control' if they feel that their child is 'not being supported appropriately or enough'. Tricia's parents were also impressed by how the school for the deaf involved a range of professionals in the Statement review process. However, Tricia's Statement had not been converted into a new EHC Plan; this was going to happen later in the year.

Learning: what and how

Provision

Tricia was doing a level 2 health and social care course at the local further education college three days a week, while the rest of her programme was done at the school for the deaf two days a week, that involved literacy, numeracy, BSL, speech therapy and pastoral support. She has a CSW who supports her on the college course, and has three hours a week CSW tutorials for one-to-one support for her college coursework.

Tricia was one of two students from the school for the deaf doing the health and social care course, but they were in different groups. Tricia explained how the classes worked for her. She was given a paper which summarized what was on the board, while the CSW signed to her what the teacher was saying. She felt this was a good way for her to learn: 'It makes me more confident.' She is taught in the school for the deaf in small groups of about five students. Her teacher also explained how they decided to change her progression on her college course several months ago. She was due to go to level 2 at the end of her first year, but because of the pressure she had been under on level 1, she was going to transfer to a work-based diploma at level 2 to be on a work placement. He explained that she might then be able to continue with the level 2 course and perhaps progress on to level 3. Tricia herself explained that this was a Functional Skills level 2, which is more like work and she was really interested in doing this.

Communicating

Tricia's teacher described that they tend to sign and speak to Tricia at the same time, because Tricia's understanding of English is higher than that of many other students due to her 'useful' hearing with a cochlea implant. He called this 'speech with signed support'. Her parents talked about having BSL evening classes and family support lessons at home. They communicated to her by a mix of speech and signing. Her father explained that they also relied on 'normal hearing' too because of her hearing aid and implant. Tricia's mother mentioned that Tricia has called her mother's BSL 'absolutely shocking'.

Both parents believed it was very important that Tricia learns to communicate with hearing people. As her father explained, 'unfortunately it's a life skill' as she was 'going to be dealing with people who have no idea of deaf awareness'. He felt it was important that people are made to be aware that 'she is deaf from an early time so they can adapt'. He also mentioned a particular person associated with the school for deaf who had a cochlea implant, someone who had been a role model for Tricia: 'she was motivated by that to have her one'.

Her parents described how the cochlea implant had made a difference to Tricia. Within one day of turning it on Tricia began to hear sounds for the first time – for example, the clock ticking and birds tweeting. Her father thought that it enabled her to hear noises around her, giving her greater social awareness. They both felt that her hearing of speech sounds was improving, though she continued to not hear some sounds, such as c and s. This is where they felt she would need continuing speech therapy. But, Tricia's mother was a little concerned that some of her deaf peers 'take down her English learning' because they were signers. They had no 'aspiration to a life outside the deaf community'.

Tricia talked about having the implant when she was 15 and that it had improved her hearing: 'I could hear birds flying for the first time.' But she also said that sometimes she 'hated college' because there was too much background noise. She described her typical communication as involving both signing and speech. With her friends, family and partner she signs, though she also does some speaking at home. But, on balance, Tricia 'prefers sign language', even though she 'does both'. She talked further about her partner who could not talk, but she said that she was 'trying to teach him to lip-read'. She explained that he hated wearing hearing aids which goes back to when he was a young child and the aids were noisy for him.

Progress, capabilities and programmes

Her parents realized that she was 'struggling with GCSE', but were concerned that the change of the GCSE back to a more exam-oriented system was not suited to her. However, her father recognized that 'she's probably got as good a thing as we could have provided for her'. They both felt that what she needed to learn was basically the same as for others who were not deaf, but that 'communication is really important'. They also saw the importance of her having 'inspiring teachers' and 'role models'.

There was common ground between her parents and teacher about the commitment she showed to her studies, but some differences in views about how far she could progress. Her teacher talked about Tricia's aspirations to reach a certain level and how her parents had encouraged her to do well at everything. Her father described Tricia as 'intellectually she's probably capable of it (a degree) given the commitment she's doing'. Her teacher described her perspective as one that believed up to this year that 'I can do this, I will do this, and I'm determined', but he wondered if her experiences on the level 1 course made her doubt how she might cope with level 2 and beyond up to 'level 6 at university'.

Lecturers and assistants

Tricia's parents saw her relationships with the staff at the school for deaf as very positive, despite finding 'some bits difficult'. They saw this as 'a significant advantage' of this kind of school where staff are 'qualified in deaf teaching and are very deaf aware socially'. Tricia also expressed her satisfaction with her lecturers who she described as very 'deaf aware'.

Her parents talked about how Tricia had learned BSL from a teaching assistant at her primary school. This woman, whose sister was deaf, was very interested in working with Tricia and eventually got herself up to level 3 in BSL. They both felt that Tricia relied on assistants a lot, her father saying that he did not think that 'she could cope without one'. At the school for the deaf Tricia had at least two CSWs as it was thought to be beneficial for her to experience different people signing. The CSWs come from different parts of the country where signing styles vary. Her teacher explained that most of the CSWs had degrees and went through a high-level intensive sign language course. Tricia herself welcomed having different CSW support. At college she tried to work on her own and if she needed help she requested it from the CSW.

What helps/hinders

Tricia's teacher believed that what helped her learn was being given 'more time on a one-to-one basis', learning in a visual way across different subject areas and using something tangible or concrete for abstract ideas, 'something that will bring it to life for them in a visual way'. He commented that as a 'very general statement', deaf people 'have a very low retention rate of theoretical information'. Her father described her as 'caring for people' and needing 'stability'. In addition, he felt that she required 'short-term' tasks to achieve. He considered that if her environment did not take her disability into account that might interfere with her learning. But, he remarked that there had been a positive working relationship between the school for the deaf and the college which had 'a very good awareness of disabilities'. Tricia's teacher also talked about how her emotional states could interfere with her learning. This he related to how she was relating to her parents and her partner, including what was going on in her partner's life.

Placement

Where at school

Tricia started out at a hearing impairment unit in a primary school some distance from her home. As this involved travelling, she was transferred to her local village school. Tricia remembers that school as 'not very good'. When she moved to her local village primary school she remembers feeling 'very lonely . . . and very sad'. She contrasted this with her current school for the deaf which she 'loved'. Tricia's mother described her primary school as 'fine', but as Tricia got older in the local primary school her friends became younger. Her peer group began to change: 'they were getting sort of teenagery' and tended to talk less to Tricia and she 'got left out'.

Her parents talked about the problems they had when she transferred to secondary school. The local comprehensive schools were 'not conducive to deafness', architecturally very badly designed, with a dearth of staff who were 'deaf aware or qualified in deafness'. Her parents did not want her 'ghettoized within a deaf community'. Initially they did not want Tricia to go to the urban school for the deaf; they wanted her to stay at a local secondary school with a unit. But, as her father explained, it did not exist within ten miles of where they lived so they realized that they had to be 'realistic about it'. There was a secondary school with a deaf unit in the urban area, but that was too far to travel every day and there were no residential facilities. They had also tried to see about a place at a grammar school for the deaf, but she did not achieve the results to be offered a place. Eventually, when her parents spoke with the staff at the school for the deaf, they 'realized it was the most practical thing we could do for her'. Once she attended this school they arranged that she comes home every weekend.

Tricia's teacher described Tricia as 'liking the bi-cultural'. He felt that her current environment 'gives her the best of both worlds – she's out there in a hearing college but she's also back here in a deaf environment as well'. He believed that the school for the deaf had a very flexible approach that caters for Tricia's needs: 'I don't think that she could be educated any other way appropriately.' Tricia herself was very pleased with her move to this school, though at first she was a 'bit scared' and felt that 'she missed her parents', but now she had 'got new friends'.

Outside school activity

Tricia's mother described how Tricia had become a Guide Leader and was taking the Duke of Edinburgh Bronze Award. Her father said that the Guide organization had helped her tremendously. This was one of the reasons for her coming home on Friday evenings. The Guides had, in her father's view, been 'superb in going out of their way to learn signing, to promote the positiveness of disability, not just deaf disability'. Tricia had been included in the widest sense in social and educational activities. In addition, Tricia went to a local deaf club in a nearby town, where she had even taken a Guide friend who had learned BSL.

Inclusion/exclusion

Tricia's father explained that he would have liked 'total inclusion', but felt that 'it's not going to happen, never will, so you have to be pragmatic about it'. Her mother backed this up by saying that 'you have to live in the real world'. Tricia's parents saw this as about distances, finance and attitudes. As her father explained: 'you can't expect the educational system to be funded to the degree that any form of disability can be inclusive'. He continued that some lucky deaf people might live near a school for the deaf, but that most will not. Tricia's mother added that she would never have thought that Tricia would go to a school for the deaf, given her views and feelings. Her father went on to explain that, for parents like them, 'at first there's denial that your child has special educational needs and needs to go to a place like that'. Both parents saw a key role for schools for the deaf for these reasons. First, fully resourced and staffed units dispersed around ordinary schools would be very expensive and hard to manage, Secondly, there is a need to 'concentrate expertise in certain areas . . . where staff are trained'.

Tricia's teacher, who had worked with deaf people for many years, believed that 'without people like himself and other colleagues they would have a really hard time out there'. He had seen many young people who started out in ordinary schools come late to the school for the deaf, and had been adversely affected by their ordinary school experiences. He was 'scared that so many (special schools) are closing'. He gave, as an example, how in one city the sensory support service had placed increasing numbers of deaf pupils in the mainstream over the last decade. He was in favour of supporting deaf students in ordinary courses at further education college. At a residential school like Tricia's, 'it gives them, especially those who don't come from deaf families, the cultural identity they need'.

Parental involvement

Relationship with teachers

Tricia's teacher talked about having regular contact with Tricia's parents through emails and phone calls. Tricia's father considered their relationship with teachers to be 'excellent'. He considered that what makes the relationship work is 'constant communication, even at a very superficial, shallow type level'. Tricia's teacher recalled no serious areas of disagreement between her parents and the school: 'they've been very positive about the support we give her'. He recalled some issues about transport that involved the local authority, but not the school.

Support groups

Tricia's parents belonged to the National Deaf Children's Society (NDCS) as well as some other disability groups. They had found the NDCS support 'tremendous'. They talked about the free helpline where they got advice about Statement issues. Tricia had also been on free holidays with the organization several times. Tricia's mother also discussed the many online forums and groups that 'you can dip in and out of depending on the issue'.

Social interaction

Tricia's teacher remarked that Tricia had become more assertive at home, and this had posed some challenges for her parents recently. He also mentioned that this had some impact on her life at school. Tricia's parents also expressed their anxieties about her as an 18-year-old, which was irrespective of whether she is 'deaf or not'. They talked about working 'quite hard to keep her having a good relationship with us'.

Tricia's teacher talked about how she had 'firm friendships' at college and 'gets on with pretty much anybody'. She is also 'well liked within her group' and 'she likes most of her fellow students', but he remarked how it is difficult for her to form friendships in her college class as she has to focus on her learning.

Tricia's mother was aware that Tricia had lost contact with a 'lot of her friends that she knew at primary school', though she still had her Guide friends. Her parents talked about her 'profoundly deaf boyfriend' who 'won't talk'. But, from what Tricia's mother said, he could not talk because he did not start talking when he was a child. Her father explained that Tricia's boyfriend had 'radical leanings' about not talking and preferred to sign.

Tricia herself talked about how she got on well with the other students in her college course who were aware that she had a hearing aid and cochlea implant. She tried to teach them to use BSL and, from what she said, they liked to try signing, even if none of them became very proficient at it. She also described how they ask her questions, but she did not spend any time with them outside classes. She explained that she 'did not mind' this, nor feel rejected, saying: 'I feel brave.' Overall, she said that she had 'very few hearing friends', most were deaf, but that her 'family is hearing . . . so I'm quite in the middle'.

Her parents appreciated that interactive social media had done very much to link Tricia to others anywhere in the world. Her father mentioned that 'deafness used to be an extremely isolating disability . . . it's not so now'. It had led her to want to travel by train to see friends, to go off on holiday, and even consider 'going to a deaf university in the United States'. Though they saw social media on balance as 'very good', her mother also saw it as cutting her off, 'because she just sits there with Facebook'; but, as her father said, 'you get that with any teenager, disabled or not'.

Tricia described how she used social media to link with her friends, using mostly Facetime and Facebook. She had contacts beyond her local area with people across the country. Some of these she met up with when she went camping with the NDCS. For her, life without social media would be 'boring'.

Future

Immediate future

Her parents felt that the outlook for her 'all things being equal, was reasonably good' given the education she had had so far and the consistent support she got from her family. But her father was uncertain about what would come after her current course, which at the time had 18 months to go. He saw that, if she achieved level 3, she could continue in further education, but he saw that this depends on 'what the government will impose . . . so we're still to find out that; it's unfortunately in flux at the moment'. Her teacher felt that the work-based diploma she was going to do next year would give her 'another year's maturity and world experience' and so she might be ready to go on to a level 3 course.

Hopes

Her father hoped that Tricia would find 'a job that will fulfil her needs and that she will enjoy doing' and 'that she has a positive relationship with somebody at some point'; similar to their son.

Her teacher thought that Tricia had a 'very bright future' compared to some of students in the school for the deaf, many of whom had 'quite severe additional needs'. He commented on her manner: 'she's got a lovely way about her; she communicates extremely well'. He felt that if she gets involved in something 'she will grasp it with both hands' and 'she'll see it to the end'. He believed that she had 'good employment prospects'. But, he had some doubts about whether, as regards her 'aspirations and dreams', 'she'll ever get there'.

Tricia talked clearly about her hopes. She wanted 'to make a new family', even though she mentioned that her parents did not 'want me to have a deaf child'. This did not bother her. She also had plans to travel with her boyfriend. She talked about the places she had visited internationally and said she wanted to travel with her friends now.

Worries

Tricia's mother worried about communicating with Tricia while her father worried about Tricia not understanding the complexity of the world. He gave, as an example, the issues about future funding for her education depending on policy decisions. This meant that they would have to 'support her probably more than their son'; that it was their job to provide a 'safety net'. For Tricia's parents a main source of fear was 'that government policy will take things away from her that she was given to expect she would have'.

Tricia's teacher talked about a possible difference in views between Tricia and her parents about her future. He saw her as becoming 'her own person' and wondered if there might be issues in her relationship with her parents over her boyfriend. When Tricia was asked about her worries about the future, she talked about university. She had heard that university is 'very hard', so she 'gets scared' because she felt that she was 'not very good at English' and needed help.

Future plans

Tricia's parents talked about her wanting to be an interpreter, deaf counsellor or teacher, perhaps a CSW. Her teacher thought she was not yet ready to pursue these occupational options; perhaps 'that is a possibility in the future'. He believed that 'she's very good with young children, she's very good with the clients at one of the centres ... they love her there'. He considered that on the basis of her practice diploma she might be offered a job at such a centre. But he saw her parents as wanting her to do more than that. When Tricia talked about her future she mentioned becoming a counsellor and travelling the world to places where there were no deaf schools. She wanted to work in deaf education in developing countries. She wondered whether she could do that without going to university. But she also wondered if she might go to university where her parents 'really want me to go'. For her, this was uncertain as she was aware that 'it's very rare for a deaf person to go to university'.

14

Lessons learned and discussion

Introduction

This final chapter takes an overview across the case study reports. It is organized in two parts: first, there is a brief summary of the kinds of advice provided by those involved in the studies (excerpts at the start of each chapter), and second, there is a more extensive discussion of some of the key themes from the range of case study reports. This will highlight some of the underlying issues that emerge and, where relevant, will be linked to current policy and practice, relevant research, and thinking in the field.

1. Lessons from participants' advice to others

The advice given by parents, teachers and young people themselves can be seen to apply to teachers and schools, on the one hand, and to parents, on the other. The most common broad theme of advice for teachers, which was given mostly by teachers themselves, was about the importance of *getting to know and understand the child or young person*. This covered: getting to know the young person really well, being person-centred, and taking time to get to know the parent and child. For one mother, it was about finding out more about how a child is different from others. One teacher talked about getting to know the young person, which also meant understanding the person's limits, which could be pushed a little. Along a similar line another teacher said that the basis for setting learning expectation was starting where the child was. Only one of the children and young people involved gave advice related to the 'getting to know' theme. George, 15 years old and with a visual impairment, believed that adults should ask what was needed and not force things on children and young people when they were not necessary.

The next most common advice theme for teachers was about *trying different things and being flexible*. Two of them talked specifically about pupils' personal differences, calling for variations in teaching strategies and approaches. There were also other kinds of advice. An advisory teacher talked about *encouraging pupils to have a go at activities*, while two assistants talked about both *calling on others for advice* and the importance of *encouraging learner independence in learning.* The only parent to refer specifically to a teaching approach was the father of Steve, who believed that adapted teaching for dyslexia was good for all and that *teaching relevant to SEN was basically about extending general teaching approaches.*

Another common theme in the advice for teachers was about *teachers needing to listen to parents to find out what they understand about their children.* This point was mentioned by the two mothers of the children with social emotional and mental health difficulties. For another parent it was about good communications between teachers and parents; keep talking, little and often. Other kinds of advice for teachers came only from teachers themselves and were about: ignoring the label to look at needs, trying to understand what has happened to the child or young person, respecting them, building a relationship with the child or young person, and finding a balance between being optimistic and realistic.

While much of the advice for teachers came from teachers themselves, several parents had specific advice for teachers too. By contrast, the advice for parents came mainly from parents themselves; only one teaching assistant had advice for parents. Eight of the twelve parents, including both mothers and fathers, advised *parents to be determined in securing the right provision for their child.* This was expressed in various ways: be as pushy as you can, do not accept provision if it did not feel right, learn how to question what is provided, be determined and do not get put off, be prepared to be disliked and be a rebel, speak up and fight for the child, and do not let them grind you down.

Three of the parents talked about expanding their understanding about disability and how to respond; thinking 'outside the box' and stretching your understanding as far as possible. The advice of three further parents was about SEN provision; that there was a *definite need for specialized placements* and *not place your child in a school where s/he was not wanted.* As, in the advice for teachers, there was only one example of advice for parents from a young person; from the young student who was deaf. She realized that her parents wanted to help her a lot, but she wanted them to know that she only wanted to be helped a little.

2.   Themes from cross-case analysis

(i) Identifying SEN and disability

Assumptions about SEN and disability

Several of the case studies brought out the distinction between describing the child or young person's difficulties in terms of a disability or disorder category or in terms of a more individualized account of their functional strengths and difficulties in relation to their context.

Marian had several functional difficulties in addition to the known brain injury. All were relevant, depending on the significance and use of the descriptions.

The cognitive and social-emotional functioning might be relevant to educational decisions and provision, while the brain injury relevant for understanding original causation. Though Marian was put into the moderate learning difficulty category for this study, this is an over-simplification and ignores the complexity and individuality of her functioning and service needs. In another case, Sandy's teaching assistant also believed that Sandy's difficulties did not fit any category.

Both Sharon and Ben had Down Syndrome diagnoses, but what was important for their wider learning and development depended on other impairments and health conditions, as well as their cognitive and self-help functioning. As Ben's mother commented, his Down Syndrome was minor compared to the other factors. The distinction between disability-disorder categories and a complex individual functional description was also evident in George's case study. His functional difficulties in school were much greater as a young child than most people understood at this stage. This was about them not recognizing the significance of his diagnosed visual impairment for his educational development. As the functional significance became evident over time, he came to settle and thrive in school. His advisory teacher believed that personal and social factors also played a major part in his school and outside school achievements.

These four cases illustrate the importance of distinguishing between medical categories, functional impairments and activity limitations, while taking account of social and environmental factors that relate to development and learning. This kind of analysis has links to the current World Health Organization framework; called the International Classification of Functioning (ICF: WHO 2007). This framework integrates elements of the medical model with its biological causes, and the social model with its environmental causes. While recognizing the place of general diagnostic categories, such as Down Syndrome or Autistic Spectrum Disorder, it also recognizes different types of personal variations in functioning (body structures and functions) that interact with personal activities and social participation that are also influenced by environmental factors.

The social factors that affected George's early school career that came to change with greater understanding of his functioning and needs also point to the importance of changing function over time. Two other case studies reinforce the significance of changes over time. The emotions and behaviour of Alex, who had a diagnosis of autism, changed over time as he settled into his schooling, experiencing less anxiety and having fewer tantrums. Julia, who had a clear diagnosis, had a progressive neurological condition which had changing functional implications over time. These cases from a perspective of change over time also show the need for a framework, such as the ICF, which focuses on changing functioning in a context.

Other cases also show how both biological and social factors are implicated in the origins of diverse areas of SEN. Steve's father, based on his own early literacy difficulties, saw dyslexia as having a strong genetic causation. Jon's mother saw Jon's difficulties as reflecting some underlying factor, even though no professional provided her with a coherent diagnosis; but she also saw his primary school as a major cause of the aggravation of his difficulties. Sandy's mother also saw Sandy's emotions and behaviours as out of her control like an illness, but saw little value in psychiatric labels.

One of the case studies illustrated how cultural assumptions affect whether a type of biological functioning (profound hearing loss) is regarded as an impairment or disability. Tricia's parents saw her as having a disability, while she saw herself sometimes as having a disability (when in a hearing cultural context) but at other times as not having a disability (when signing with other deaf young people). Her case reflects issues and questions dealt with in other studies about bi-culturalism and the deaf community (Skelton and Valentine, 2003).

Value of identification

For six of the twelve case studies the value of identification was assumed, while for the other six cases the value of identification was an issue. In at least two cases the use of disorder categories was seen as pragmatic from the parents' perspective. Ben's mother had considered whether Ben might get an autism diagnosis in addition to his other diagnoses, but decided to wait and judged this in terms of whether it added anything to accessing of relevant provision. This pragmatic parental perspective has been illustrated in other related research about parents (Russell and Norwich, 2012). Steve's parents were critical of professionals for not using the dyslexia term, nor communicating with them about the severity of Steve's difficulties. They saw this as motivated by a reluctance to take responsibility for funding provision. But they also saw the identification as the way to access resources.

Jon's mother sought some way of identifying his difficulties to help her in coping with Jon, despite various categories being considered but not seen as relevant by various professionals. This contrasted with Sandy's mother who strongly rejected various labels used by mental health and other professionals, such as ADHD, ODD and attachment disorder. For her, labels were damaging and a distraction from consistent and effective provision.

For four other cases, there were differing degrees of ambivalence about the use and value of labels from different perspectives. Steve's teacher was uncertain about the value of the term 'dyslexia' for teaching, but did see it as useful for understanding experiences of difficulties. This connects with current perspectives about the different purposes of labels (Laughlin and Boyle, 2007). Steve believed that he had special educational needs, but did not feel that he had a disability, a term he associated with physical disabilities. Alex's mother also believed that the ASD label helped her to understand Alex's needs, but she and her husband did not let Alex (age 9) know about the diagnosis and label – at least not yet. By contrast, Nina who was 18 years old, was aware of her autism, according to her mother, and experienced some conflict between positive and negative aspects. George, another teenage participant, recognized that he had a visual impairment, but did not like to be marked out socially as having this impairment.

Some of the above tensions can be seen to reflect conflicts between positive and negative aspects of identification and labelling, which can lead those involved to experience dilemmas about their difference (Norwich, 2008a). The dilemmas of difference can be experienced from different perspectives, as shown in these case studies. As dilemmas they involve hard or risky choices about using specific categories or labels in terms of understanding a condition and accessing relevant provision versus experiencing negative treatment and/or feeling negative emotions. Those experiencing tensions or dilemmas resolve them by weighing up the pros and cons and finding a workable balance for themselves. This process is also illustrated in some of the case studies. Nina's mother recognized that using the autism category was useful for resourcing as this was what counted. Similarly, George's parents came to accept a visual impairment label to open resource doors.

Impact

A consistent theme across the cases was about how hard it was to deal with their experiences of SEN/disability. In three cases the same term 'devastated' was used to describe the emotional impact on their mothers. Impacts were identified in at least one case on work, family lifestyle, personal health and siblings (Ludlow, Skelly and Rohleder, 2012). The impact on family life and relationships was described across some cases as reducing child contact with fathers, separation, and not having another child. Four of the teenagers involved were described as having experienced sadness or frustrations at some times, related to their condition. But, in only two of the 12 cases, were some positive aspects described. Sharon's father described how Sharon's difficulties had brought them closer to their wider family. Ben's mother talked about his condition releasing them from social pressures, enabling them to make good friends and undertake new activities.

Others' responses

Several cases show a pattern of mixed and changing responses over time. In Ben, George and Tom's cases, early negative experiences from others changed to more positive ones as other children came to accept them. Staring was an example of a negative experience mentioned specifically in two cases. Mothers feeling blamed for their child's behaviour problems was another in three cases, with the assumption that the mothers were bad parents. There were also single cases which focused more on the negative responses from others or where there were few experiences of negative responses.

Statements/Plans

There were two cases where there were only minor issues experienced about the process of issuing Statements of Special Educational Needs. In two-thirds of the cases there were difficulties either in securing a Statement in the first instance or in the Statement enabling access to specific kinds of provision or resources. Reluctance to issue Statements when requested did eventually lead to the issuing of a Statement, but not without what parents saw as a battle or fight. Confrontations were over access to speech and language therapy, travel and resources when transferring from primary to secondary school. There was an example of one parent not being told about available support that could be requested. Another case reflected how the Statement process reflected tensions over placement decisions, rather than being a process that helped resolve the issues.

These kinds of issues have been widely documented in the literature, as well as policy documents (Lamb Inquiry Report: DFE (2009). These sources also indicate that parents saw the value in the protections provided by the Statement system, as did those who participated in the case studies. Several of the parents in the case studies believed that they would have got nowhere without a Statement. However, their support was for the principle rather than the practices associated with Statements. This was evident in the specific criticisms expressed, even by parents who supported the protection principle. These included having to overemphasize their children's difficulties to secure required provision; that the process was more about funding than personal programme planning for their child; that Statement reports were very vague; and that the process was complex and excessively bureaucratic. These perspectives can be interpreted as consistent with a policy of using the legal protection of a Statement or Plan when parents require it, not as the standard approach to deciding on provision for all pupils with significant special educational needs (Warnock, Norwich and Terzi, 2010).

The experience of the parents in this study showed that few had been involved in the new system of EHC Plans. Of the ten parents who had Statements, only one had been converted to a Plan, while another was in a delayed process of conversion. Jon was about to start the statutory process for the issuing of an EHC plan. The one parent who had a Plan noticed no difference from the previous Statement, while two parents whose children had severe learning difficulties and additional care needs liked the principle of bringing together education, health and care into the planning system.

(ii) Mental health aspects

For three of the twelve cases mental health issues were central to their experiences. Marian's mother found that, in seeking mental health support about coping with Marian, she could only access individual support if she first took part in a parent training course. She found this very insulting and as indicating how the system made her feel that she was to blame for how Marian behaved. For Jon, who was at an alternative provision setting, there were continuing issues for his mother to secure mental health support for him. She had repeatedly asked for help before he started school, but he only accessed therapeutic-style activities (Thrive) when he started in the reception year of primary school. However, these were significantly reduced because Jon was said to be a risk to others. Sandy's mother had a very low opinion of mental health support. For her, everyone got involved at some point, but little happened or changed that was positive. She preferred therapy and environmental-style intervention for Sandy rather than drug treatments. She had also been offered a parenting course.

(iii) Learning: what and how

Attitude to school/college provision

Overall, most of the parents were positive about their children's schooling or college provision (six of the twelve). In three further instances parents became positive after initial problems. In one case this was about recognizing the nature and degree of the visual impairment (George). In the second, a more positive attitude followed transfer from a primary school that struggled for several years to a responsive special school (Sharon). The third case followed a similar positive attitude change following transfer, but from a primary school to private school with a dyslexia unit (Steve). In a further case, the parent was satisfied with the residential special school and appreciated what the primary school had provided (Sandy). There were two further cases where parents were dissatisfied with provision, and they both also involved mental health service aspects (Jon and Marian).

This analysis illustrates the wider national issues about child and adolescent mental health services and the relationships between these and educational services. For example, the House of Commons Health Select Committee report (House of Commons, 2014) called for the Department of Education to coordinate policy in this field (see recent DFE guidance to schools on mental health matters: DFE, 2014a). A further point that arises from the cross-case analysis was that parental satisfaction/dissatisfaction varied with the capability/lack of capability of a primary school to accommodate a child with a severe learning (intellectual) difficulty (Sharon compared to Ben). Both had had part-time placements in a special school during their time at primary school, but one transferred early to special school through dissatisfaction with provision, while the other went through primary school which was seen as satisfactory and transferred to a special school co-located with a secondary school.

Teaching approaches and settings

The various teaching approaches used with case study pupils/students need to be seen in the context of the settings in which teaching took place. The case study settings range along what has come to be called a continuum of provision:

- *Ordinary class only*: (George) with advisory teacher support and teaching assistant support as requested by pupil.
- *Ordinary class and access to rest room*: (Julia) physical adaptations in primary and secondary schools and opportunity to access withdrawal rest room.
- *Ordinary class and additional sessions outside usual lesson time*: (Tom) with speech and language centre teaching assistant support; (Alex) with teaching assistant support.

- *Ordinary class and some withdrawal during lessons*: (Marian) in-class teaching assistant support and withdrawal; (Steve) ordinary subject lessons and withdrawal to dyslexia centre, in ordinary residential school.
- *Mainly withdrawal, some ordinary class*: (Sandy) with teaching assistant when at primary school; (Ben) in-class for topic work with TA; one-to-one at other times with assistant.
- *Return to younger age group and part-time special placement*: (Sharon) went to reception year, though older and part-time in special school before moving to special school; (Ben) to reception year, part-time in special school.
- *Separate specialist settings and ordinary setting*: (Tricia) vocational course in further education college and special college teaching.
- *Separate setting full time*: (Jon) Alternative provision setting following exclusion and limited tutorial; (Nina) residential specialist college; (Sandy) residential special school.

The above summary shows that the traditional continuum of placement defined by the increasing distance from ordinary classrooms (Deno, 1970) has become more complex with greater variations including the combination of settings, movement of pupils to different year groups, special units in residential ordinary school and the central role of teaching assistants inside and outside ordinary classes.

Teaching approaches

- Adaptations of access: Julia (motor), George (visual).
- Specific teaching strategies: Marian (precision teaching, concrete tasks); Sandy (treat each day as fresh start).
- Personalized goals across curriculum: Sharon, Jon, Ben.
- Building confidence/self-esteem: Steve.
- Therapeutic approaches: Jon (Thrive), Tom (speech therapy), Sandy.
- Literacy and numeracy embedded in life and social skills: Nina.
- Responsive to pupil's support wishes: George, Julia.
- Alternative signing/communicating system: Tom and Sharon (Makaton), Julia (British Sign Language).

Analysis of teaching approaches across the case studies in the box above shows the rich mixture of the varied kinds of teaching approaches used with this range of children and young people with SEN and disabilities. Much could be written about this, but for the purposes of this chapter, it is notable that the kinds of approaches reported by participants relate to the specific kinds of individual functioning, rather than the broad categories of SEN.

In addition, two teaching principles were suggested by some participants. One was about how teaching decisions strike a balance between potentially contrary aims – for example, doing what a teacher or assistant saw as needed, versus encouraging the pupil to be independent and manage her/himself. This kind of teaching dilemma is discussed further in Norwich (2008a). The other principle was that special or specialist teaching was not that different from general teaching approaches and could be seen as an extension and adaptation of such approaches. This was in line with ideas about a continuum of teaching approaches or strategies as developed by Lewis and Norwich (2004).

Teaching principles

- Balance between what is needed and managing himself: Alex, George, Julia.
- Specialized teaching as extension of general teaching approaches: Steve, Alex, Ben.

Teaching and other assistants

In five of the twelve cases, parents reported that their main school link was with the teaching assistant, rather than the class teacher of their child. Parents suggested assistants rather than a teacher to interview in four cases, three of whom were mentioned by parents as their main link. In four of the five where the assistant was the main link with school, parents also felt that the assistant seemed to assume more responsibility for their child than the class teacher.

In three cases parents were very satisfied and impressed with the support work done by the assistant, while in four cases parents had some dissatisfaction, whether about the quality of support, knowing enough about how support was given or that their child relied too much on the assistant. Four of the children or young people themselves had mixed feelings about their teaching assistant support, mainly about them being marked out negatively by having this support. In one case the child (Jon) tended to have very strong emotional attachments to his assistants. What these findings suggest can be interpreted in terms of recent research about the risks and advantages of teaching assistants in the support of pupils with SEN/disabilities (Blatchford, Russell and Webster, 2012) and also seen in light of recent guidance about deploying teaching assistants (Sharples, Webster and Blatchford, 2015).

(iv) *Where at school and college*

Placement experiences and preferences

Many of the parents and some teachers and assistants were clear about their reasons for not opting for a special school placement. Some saw the separation as less than ideal, though sometimes necessary under some conditions – for example, for severe behaviour difficulties or additional complex and care needs. Others were opposed to the pupils spending time only with those with similar difficulties or disabilities. Another common reason for opposing special schools was the travelling distance from where they lived.

Various reasons were given for transfer to special schools or colleges that were about issues in ordinary settings. The struggles to secure appropriate accommodations for Sharon led her parents, despite their inclinations, to opt for special school. Another mother rejected an ordinary further education college setting given issues experienced in this kind of setting when Nina was at a special school. Another mother recognized that her son might not cope in a primary school and was open to professional advice about the advantages of a separate setting. The idea that special school might become more appropriate for secondary schooling was also a common theme across these cases.

A clear pattern of preference was shown in six of the twelve case studies for special or resource units or centres in ordinary school settings. This was evident in a wide range of SEN areas. There was only one reference to negative aspects of such units. Another feature of preferred placements was combined (special and ordinary settings) or co-located settings (special settings on the same campus as ordinary settings). It is notable that, despite these preferences, there are very few references to what units/centres can contribute to meeting needs and satisfying parental preferences in the new SEN Code of Practice (DFE, 2014b). The same applies to co-located and combined special-ordinary placements. An earlier report by Ofsted (2006) indicated some benefits of special needs units in ordinary schools in terms of pupil outcomes, but since then there has been little research or development in this area of provision.

Attitudes and beliefs about separate/special settings

Overall, parents, teachers and teaching assistants preferred provision for children and young people with significant SEN/disabilities in ordinary schools with support, where the child will cope and thrive and the school had the commitment and expertise to support the pupil. Some parents were dissatisfied with schools not showing enough commitment to making provision work for their children. However, most of them could also see the value of separate special schools under some circumstances, such as those discussed in the above section.

A few parents and teachers explained how they were initially very supportive of a fully inclusive school system where there would be no special schools, but came to see the value of special schools sometimes with a sense disappointment.

This was framed as a matter of realism or pragmatism about what ordinary schools could or were willing to do, and the cost of dispersed units staffed by skilled professionals, amongst other factors. Julia's mother, for example, talked about having your child in an ordinary school might look inclusive, but not be so. Nina's mother made the distinction between ordinary adaptations that could and should be made at primary phase, but not at secondary phase of schooling. She justified her belief in special schools in terms of Nina as a teenager feeling more comfortable amongst other young people with SEN/disabilities than other teenagers. This reflects the preference of some people with disabilities to associate with others similar to themselves, which can come into conflict with inclusive practices (Koutsouris, 2014). Two teachers who worked in special schools held strong views about ordinary schools holding on to children with SEN/disabilities for too long, producing negative effects for the pupils when they finally entered special schools. The nuances in the held beliefs about inclusion and special schools were reflected in the beliefs of a very experienced and accomplished teaching assistant, who though she believed in special school for some pupils, talked about striving to include some hard to include cases, if they could benefit from it. She felt that she knew more about how to achieve this given recent knowledge and experience about inclusive practices.

There were two cases where experiencing hard choices and the experienced need to balance some options were discussed. Jon's mother talked directly about getting him what he needed in a special setting and not knowing whether ordinary school placement could be made to work. The teenager George was also aware of the need to balance the positive sides of inclusion in his secondary school with the help he also needed. He felt that he had achieved a balance that worked for him; that he was as included as much as he wanted to be. These directly reported experiences, and the tensions implicit in the beliefs and attitudes expressed by other case study participants, can be seen to reflect a dilemma of difference about special setting/school placement; a choice about risks associated with both choices. As argued elsewhere, these tensions and their resolutions reflect some of the key issues in the special needs and inclusive education field (Norwich, 2008b; Norwich, 2013).

Future hopes and worries

Four of the twelve parents expressed how hard it was for them to consider the future for their children. This was associated with various factors which will be illustrated in some of the themes discussed below. For three parents of children with learning difficulties the special school community provides some hope and confidence for the future. This was associated with being in a caring context and a sense that belonging to that community settled matters for some time to come, especially for children who were in their early teenage years or younger. The idea that this kind of context could also support the parent was also expressed.

Worries about the availability of future support for their children was expressed by half of the interviewed parents. For the young people who were in secondary or post-school settings, the issues were about possible future changes in post-school funding which some parents linked to uncertainties of government policies. For children who were in primary school or transferring to secondary school, this was less about the funding as such, than about the right kind of support being available to meet personal needs.

For some parents the key worries were about whether they could protect their children in the future. Sharon's parents had concerns about protecting her against the shunning she might experience from others when she becomes a young adult. Nina's teacher could envisage an enriched life for Nina as a young adult, but she believed that she would always need help. Tom's mother was concerned about his vulnerability and the risks of bullying, as he was transferring from a special centre to an ordinary primary school.

Two mothers expressed concerns about the longer-term future, when they were no longer able to care for their children as adults. This was expressed by them setting up a trust fund and involving members of their families to organize future care for their children.

In three case studies where the additional needs were linked to a changing condition, parents had concerns about how the deterioration of the condition might affect the future. For Julia this was about her motor functioning and health, while for Jon and Sandy, who both had ongoing mental health difficulties, it was about whether the difficulties would respond to intervention or deteriorate.

Several of the children had moved at some stage from ordinary to a special school or unit setting. In only one case study was this possible transfer a future possibility, as Marian moved towards the end of primary school.

For four of the six secondary aged pupils the question of qualifications was an important future hope or issue. For Tricia there were questions of whether she would achieve some formal qualifications, go to university, or go down a vocational route. She herself expressed concern about whether she could cope at university; her parents had encouraged her to go to university, but her teacher had some doubts. There were shared hopes that Steve, despite his literacy difficulties, would achieve his five GCSE 5 A–C grades and then do something more vocational. There were clear expectations that Julia would achieve high-level GCSE qualifications and then go on to to equine studies, given her love of horses. Expectations and hope were high for George to attend university and manage a professional type of job.

Five of the twelve children and young people had quite clear ideas about what future work they might do. It was interesting that this was not confined to the older participants. Steve, George and Julia, who were older, had specific ideas – for example, being a physical education teacher or working outdoors, video game designer and yachting or studying about horses. But Sandy and Alex who were younger, also had ideas, if less clearly articulated. Sandy talked about being a paramedic or fireperson, while Alex wanted to be an engineer and design planes.

Concluding comments

This chapter has selected some of the key cross-case themes to illustrate two aspects that emerge. The first is the direct kinds of advice that parents and teachers give about what is important, and what lessons they have learned to improve practice. The second is the commentary of how the cross-case analysis of participants' experiences connect with current thinking, theories, policy and research in the field.

As the aim of this book is to provide a narrative account of experiences of special educational needs and disability, I will conclude with a summary analysis of what participants advised others as regards lessons for practice. Table 1

Table 1 Summary of parent and teacher advice.

By parents for:	
Parents	*Teachers*

1 Be determined to secure the right provision for your child, by:
  • Being 'pushy'.
  • Questioning what is offered.
  • Not being put off.
  • Being prepared to be disliked.
2 Expand your understanding of SEN and disability, by:
  • Stretching your understanding.
  • Thinking outside of the box.
3 There is a definite place for some separate specialist settings.
	1 Listen to parents and learn from them.
	2 Teaching SEN is basically extending general teaching approaches:
	  • Father who had dyslexia about teaching his son with dyslexia.

By teachers and teaching assistants for:	
Parents	*Teachers*

Communicate any concerns to school staff.	1 Get to know the child and young person by:
	  • Doing so really well.
	  • Being person-centred.
	  • Taking time to get to know the parent and child.
	  • Finding out how the child/young person is different from others.
	  • Understanding the person's limits, which could be pushed at a little.

By young person for:	
Parents	*Teachers*
More independence/self-help.	Wanted to be asked if needed help.

summarizes this advice and shows that teachers provided advice mainly for teachers and parents for parents. While only one teaching assistant felt confident to give advice to parents, some parents were confident to give advice to teachers. The most common advice by parents for other parents was about asserting their right to secure the appropriate provision for their children. Some parents urged other parents to expand their understanding of their children's needs and to recognize the value of separate special provision. Parents' advice to teachers was mainly about listening and learning from parents. Only one parent ventured to advise teachers about teaching, advice that teaching pupils with SEN was about extending general teaching approaches, which is notably consistent with the teaching principle arising from the cross-case analysis above, and a contemporary view about specialization of SEN teaching. Parents' advice to teachers to listen and learn from parents was also consistent with the main advice given by teachers to other teachers of pupils with SEN: get to know the child and young person. These messages represent simple, consistent and powerful pointers to lessons that can be learned from these case studies. Table 1 also shows the advice from two young people to parents and teachers, both of which are about teenagers wanting more self-help.

This book focuses on particular situations, practices and experiences. This is meant to contrast with books which focus on general approaches, whether they are theories and explanations or practical implications and guidance. The point of this book is to speak to the readers' interest in particular children and young people, their lives, learning and wider experiences, to engage with their stories at the level of feelings and to expand empathy to better connect readers to current thinking and practice. In engaging with thinking and theory the book has been written from a particular perspective about the education of children and young people with special educational needs and disabilities. It is the perspective that their education, like the education of all children and young people, involves a range of distinct goals and values. All these goals and values are important, but sometimes they can come into conflict and there needs to be some balancing or trade-offs between them. The experiences reflected in these case studies can be seen to illustrate some of these tensions and the dilemmas – hard choices or a choice between risks – that need to be confronted and addressed by parents, teachers and policymakers. There are established ways of resolving these tensions, many of which have also been illustrated in these case studies as well, such as having co-located special schools or special units or centres in ordinary schools. There is also scope for creativity to find other resolutions to these dilemmas. This is the understanding that has underpinned this study and my drive to complete the project presented here.

Appendix

Though the case studies were conducted in a rigorous and systematic way, they are not presented in this book in the usual format found in academic papers. This appendix gives some further details of the methods used to conduct the case studies.

Deciding on who to invite to participate in the case studies

Most of the details about how the participants came to be chosen were explained in Chapter 1. In this section I comment on some of the dimensions of differences represented in the table of participants in the study (page 4).

The initial plan was to involve 14 children and young people, but the scale was reduced to 12 for practical reasons of time and access. It was decided that this did not affect the diversity of age, gender, areas of SEN and school placements represented. Participants were sought using the conventional classification of SEN as this has been, and continues to be, the term used by parents and professionals. As argued in the book, this does not assume that the categories are valid or useful in practice. As the case reports and the final chapter discussion indicate, the focus on primary areas of SEN/disability has questionable value. The age range of participants and their educational placements represent the school and further education college phases of education provision. The pre-school and higher education phases, which are now, in principle, covered by the new legislation (the 0–25 scope) were not included, again mainly for practical reasons, but also because this book is mainly for the education and training of schoolteachers. Nevertheless, the cases do represent the continuum of provision and placements in the system and include children and young people in transition between placements.

Meeting parents

Parents who took part in the study were contacted through sending out an information and request letter. Contacts were made through writing to voluntary organizations concerned with different areas of SEN/disability, by contacting special schools and special centres, though parent groups, by attending support groups and talking to parents, parent information and advice services, local authority SEN advisory services, and individual contacts. Some parents who initially showed an interest did not wish to take part because of the risk that interviews might arouse bad experiences they wished to avoid. It was clear that parents who did want to take part were ones who wanted to express their views and saw the aims of the book as providing a way for them to communicate their experiences to others. This means that the participants are a self-selected group.

Methodological perspective

The methodological approach focused on the particularity of each case, but seen within a flexible general framework about the field. This framework was designed to maintain the primary education focus of the study, while also taking account of health and care aspects, covering the six broad themes outlined in Chapter 1, and by which each study is organized: i. identification, ii. learning: what and how, iii. placement, iv. parental involvement, v. social interaction and vi. futures. The study is driven by an interest in illustrating and providing insights into the lived experience of those involved, especially the parents of children and young people with SEN/disability.

Interview schedules were designed using a hierarchical focusing methodology (Tomlinson, 1989) that starts by setting out a conceptual map of the areas to be explored. The starting point for this map was the six areas above. From this map three versions of a semi-structured interview schedule were designed. These overlapped in coverage as much as possible, but were adapted for the participant roles, and wording was altered according to the age of the child and young person.

Interviews took place in various places depending on what suited participants. Parents were often interviewed at home, while teachers and pupils/students at school or college. Children and young people were often interviewed with an assistant present, but not in all cases. Interviews were audio recorded and fully transcribed.

Transcriptions were analysed at a case level using the NVivo programme in terms of the initial six broad areas and the emergent sub-areas that arose from making sense of the transcripts. Excerpts from the three transcripts (parent–teacher/assistant–child/young person) were sorted into common themes (nodes). The structure and content of the thematic analysis was then copied into a Word file. This was usually between 30–45 pages and was the basis for the further analysis and reduction which led to the final case studies making up the chapters of this book. The case studies have been written in a narrative style, with much use of reported experiences and views using participants' own words.

Draft copies of the case accounts were checked with participants to enhance consistency and trustworthiness of the final case. Some parents asked for minor changes, while other participants commented that the reports 'reflected the journey the child and her/his parents have been on'.

Ethical matters

The study satisfied the ethics standards for educational research, and was endorsed by the ethics committee in the University of Exeter, College of Social Science and International Studies. Participants were ensured informed consent to take part, that they could withdraw at any point in the study, and that all participants, organizations and locations will be anonymous. Data was stored in secure computer and recording systems. Nevertheless, there have been a few instances where the final case accounts have had to be written in a way that took account of the sensitivities of other participants. For example, a parent might have said something critical of a teacher who was to read the case account. Or, a parent might not have wanted their child to read something said in an interview that affected the child. This did not happen often. Where there were significant tensions in parent–teacher relations the teachers involved were not interviewed.

Strengths and limitations of study

Participants were interested in communicating their experiences. This means that the case studies are probably based on open and honest accounts. The three perspectives on each case were compared for consensus, which lends weight to the interpretations made of their experiences and perspectives. The study design reflects more emphasis on depth than breadth. This was evident in the self-selected nature of the participants group and in not involving parents from ethnic minority backgrounds. This calls for caution about generalizing what is found in these case studies. What is presented is illustrative and illuminative, rather than lending itself to simple generalization.

References

Blatchford, P., Russell, A. and Webster, R. (2012) *Reassessing the impact of teaching assistants: How research challenges practice and policy.* Oxon: Routledge.

Deno, E. (1970) Special education as developmental capital. *Exceptional Children, 37*: 229–37.

DFE (2009) *Lamb Inquiry: Special educational needs and parental confidence.* 01143-2009DOM-EN. Nottingham: DCSF.

DFE (2014a) *Mental health and behaviour in schools: Departmental advice for school staff.* London: DFE-00435-2014.

DFE (2014b) *Special educational needs and disability code of practice: 0 to 25 years: Statutory guidance for organisations who work with and support children and young people with special educational needs and disabilities.* London: DFE.

DFE/DOH (2014) *Special educational needs and disability code of practice: 0 to 25 years.* London: DFE-00205-2013.

House of Commons (2014) *Health Select Committee Report: Children's and adolescents' mental health and CAMHS.* HC 342.

Koutsouris, G. (2014) Young people's preferences for social interaction in terms of homophily and social inclusion: a critical discussion about respect. *European Journal of Special Needs Education,* 29(4): 521–35.

Laughlin, F. and Boyle, C. (2007) Is the use of labels in special education helpful? *Support for Learning,* 22: 36–42.

Lewis, A. and Norwich, B. (eds) (2004) *Special Teaching for Special Children?: Pedagogies for Inclusion.* Maidenhead: Open University Press.

Ludlow, A., Skelly, C. and Rohleder, P. (2012) Challenges faced by parents of children diagnosed with autism spectrum disorder. *Journal of Health Psychology,* 17(5): 702–11.

Norwich, B. (2008a) *Dilemmas of difference, inclusion and disability: International perspectives and future directions.* London: Routledge.

Norwich, B. (2008b) What future for special schools and inclusion? conceptual and professional perspectives.. *British Journal of Special Education,* 35(3): 136–44.

Norwich, B. (2013) *Addressing tensions and dilemmas in inclusive education: Living with uncertainty.* London: Routledge.

Ofsted (2006) *Inclusion: does it matter where pupils are taught? Provision and outcomes in different settings for pupils with learning difficulties and disabilities.* HMI 2535.

Russell, G. and Norwich, B. (2012) Dilemmas, diagnosis and de-stigmatization: parental perspectives on autistic spectrum disorders. *Clinical Child Psychology and Psychiatry,* 17(2): 229–45.

Sharples, J., Webster, R. and Blatchford, P. (2015) *Making Best Use of Teaching Assistants: Guidance report.* London: Educational Endowment Foundation.

Skelton, T. and Valentine, G. (2003) 'It feels like being deaf is normal': an exploration into the complexities of defining D/deafness and young D/deaf people's identities. *The Canadian Geographer,* 47(4): 451–66.

Tomlinson, P. (1989) Having it Both Ways: hierarchical focusing as research interview method. *British Educational Research Journal,* 15(2): 155–76.

Warnock, M., Norwich, B. and Terzi, L. (2010) *Special Educational Needs a New Look.* London: Continuum Books.

WHO (2007) *International Classification of Functioning, Disability and Health – Children and Youth version.* Geneva: WHO. Available at: http://apps.who.int/iris/bitstream/10665/43737/1/9789241547321_eng.pdf (accessed 17 March 2016).

Index